TERRY ANNE WILSON & JO PARFITT

MONDAY MORNING EMAILS

D1606393

Six months, twelve countries, a thousand thoughts — two mothers share the journey of living a global life

with Lesley Lewis, Ian Moody, Becky Grappo, Ellen Mahoney, Colleen Reichrath-Smith, Ruth Van Reken, Amanda Graham and Nell Smith

ISBN 978-1-909193-97-0

Designed by creationbooth.com

Edited by Joshua Parfitt and Ginny Philps

Proofread by Paddy Hartnett

Cover concept by The Wilsons

Cover images by iStockphoto and Trixie Pacis

Letter graphic by Shutterstock.com

To Bruce, Ian, Sam, Luke, Joshua, Matt and Andrew – for sharing the journey.

We would not have had it any other way.

MONDAY MORNING EMAILS

ACKNOWLEDGEMENTS

We have many people to thank for their help with this book, first and foremost, our families. Although we were hopeful they would encourage our vision of writing so frankly, we are grateful they agreed to support us in sharing our family experiences. It is a challenge to be vulnerable, open and honest, when so many of us work hard at creating an outer persona – in the way we dress, with our homes and lifestyle, even our social media presence. Yet we recognised that a warts-and-all, take-us-as-you-find-us truthfulness would be necessary if we were to achieve our goal – that of inspiring, supporting, and helping others who may be experiencing the same issues.

Without the help of our eight wonderful experts, Becky Grappo, Ruth Van Reken, Ellen Mahoney, Amanda Graham, Nell Smith, Lesley Lewis, Ian Moody and Colleen Reichrath-Smith, we would not have come close to that goal. We thank them for their patience and working with a tight deadline when submitting their expert, insightful advice. We are inordinately grateful for their support of our project and how they embraced it.

We also thank the team who put the book together. Joshua Parfitt and Ayla Slanina for reviewing the entire manuscript. To all of our guys who offered support, editorial advice, and to the Wilson clan for book design concept. Ginny Philps for editing and production. Graham Booth for design/layout and Jack Scott for pressing the final buttons that make the book available for sale in print and digital formats worldwide.

Lastly, we are thankful for this opportunity as friends and as writers. Monday became a treasured day… we still miss opening our laptops, reading our 'letter' and creating our heartfelt responses. Yes, most definitely, we encourage the healing and the joy of writing!

Jo Parfitt and Terry Anne Wilson, The Hague and Bangalore, January 2018

CONTENTS

MONDAY MORNING EMAILS

PREFACE

Many years ago, Jo read a book called *Writing in a Convertible with the Top Down* by Christi Killien and Sheila Bender. The book, part memoir and part inspiration for writers, comprised a series of letters penned between the two friends. Written from their homes in different parts of the US, Jo loved how open and honest the writers had been. Impressed with how they discussed the issues they faced as writers and as mothers, Jo dreamed of writing her own *Convertible* one day.

In 2009 her eldest son left for university in London, while Jo, her husband Ian and their youngest son, stayed in The Hague. Two years later and now with both boys away, Jo's nest was empty. Throwing herself headlong into working 10-hour days along with a complete house renovation, the result was a burnout. A year later Jo and Ian moved to Malaysia while the boys remained in Europe. Joshua, the eldest, quit university and nine months later had a breakdown. Jo blamed herself. Isn't that a natural response for a parent? Perhaps it was because the boys were Third Culture Kids (TCKs), or was it because she and Ian had moved at a critical time? Or was it that they had not provided a family home in their passport country of England? As time went on, the challenge of an empty nest and many more issues associated with global living (but not exclusive to it) assumed greater and greater significance.

In March 2017 at the Families in Global Transition (FIGT) Conference in The Hague, Jo put together a forum on the Expat Empty Nest. Terry Anne Wilson, Becky Grappo, Ellen Mahoney and Ruth Van Reken sat on the panel. With a packed turnout, everyone in the room was in agreement that this was a significant topic, yet many other pertinent issues were raised. The panel agreed that they wanted to be involved in some way, but how?

Just before the conference that March, Jo and Ian had relocated to The Hague, while Terry Anne had been living in Bangalore for one year. On a Skype call they discussed ways forward, bouncing ideas back and forth but nothing felt quite right. It can be like that with a book, but then you just know in your gut when you hit on the right idea. Sometimes you never reach that pivotal moment. But that day in late April as Jo sat on the pale blue Ikea sofa in the living-dining-office-kitchen of their tiny transit apartment, she had an idea.

"What if we just wrote each other emails?" she suggested and watched the screen.

Terry Anne seated at her desk in her Bangalore apartment, ethereal aqua painting on the wall behind her, didn't miss a beat. "I like that. And there's no question we both have so much to share."

"I'll write to you once a week, say on a Monday, and you reply the following Monday," Jo offered.

"We'll call them our 'Monday Morning Emails'," Terry Anne continued. "I think it's a great idea!"

"But are you alright with being vulnerable?" Jo asked. "This must be truthful." She realised it was a lot to ask, but knew that if this was to work, honesty and vulnerability were key.

Things fell into place as the months went on, as the emails revealed more and more. What began as an expatriate empty nest project became more involved over time as the 'discussion' grew organically. Vital, heartfelt issues arose: parenting Adult Third Culture Kids (ATCKs), mental health, retirement dilemmas, ageing parents, identity, career, self-care and more. Jo and Terry Anne then asked their expert panellists to comment and add their professional advice.

The result is *Monday Morning Emails*. The book is indeed honest, and true.

MONDAY MORNING EMAILS

HOW TO READ THIS BOOK

This book is a combination of personal emails and expert opinions that address the pertinent subjects discussed within the correspondence. Also included are highly valuable methodologies and tools to help readers understand and embrace expatriate challenges, and a rich bibliography of further reading and resources.

We have specifically placed the majority of the expert advice in a separate section so as to avoid interrupting the flow of the emails. We hope that, according to need and mood, readers may enjoy the book as either a poetic and descriptive novel, a reference guide, and/ or a working manual to help them better understand and thrive within the expatriate adventure.

x

MONDAY MORNING EMAILS

MONDAY MORNING EMAILS

Monday, May 1, Babylon Toren, The Hague, The Netherlands

Dear Terry Anne,

It's funny how knowing that we were going to start a weekly email correspondence filled me with anticipation. I have always loved writing letters. I had pen pals when I was young. Marie-Laurence, then Marie-Pierre in France, Anne-Marie in Finland, Tini in Germany and Tom in America. During the school holidays, I would write to my friends and send postcards. When university friends moved away to start their lives I wrote to them often, wherever they lived in the world. When Ian moved to Dubai after we had been dating for a year, I lovingly wrote to him. And when in 1997 Ian and I married and I joined him in Dubai, my mother and I kept up a weekly correspondence, first by letter, then by fax, then email, and now rather pathetically by WhatsApp. More often, sure, but our messages are short, devoid of emotion and though we ping back and forth, can hardly be called conversations.

Years ago, I read a book called *Writing in a Convertible With the Top Down* by Sheila Bender and Christi Killien. This too was regular correspondence, by letter, between two writers. I always dreamed of having a similar communication and here we are. I have no idea where it will go, nor what we will discuss. Unlike Bender and Killien, our focus is not our lives as writers but our lives as fifty-something expatriates with five sons (three for you, two for me), almost 60 years abroad and 15 countries between us. Moreover, we are still overseas, our sons are in their twenties, mostly done with their studies and moving towards their own independence and adulthood.

As I write now, I realise the once so familiar art of letter-writing feels a little awkward under my fingers. I used to write pages and pages and simply let it flow. Today, I am not quite sure where this writing will lead but I am excited.

Less than six months ago we heard we were leaving Kuala Lumpur earlier than expected and would return to The Hague, from whence we had come, in the spring. We arrived in March and the company has put us up in a transit flat for three months while we sort out what comes next. Normally our posting has been for approximately four years but this time Ian's contract is for just two. This makes me feel very vulnerable. By the time we are settled it will be time to move on. Or will it? Will it be extended or will he lose his job in the meantime? The Hague is the one place in the world where we own a property. We've been lucky, renting it out to a chap who has been looking after it the entire time we have been in Malaysia. The only trouble is that the law, of course, is on the side of the tenant and despite our constant queries as to whether he may leave before his contract is up in November, or whether he wants to extend it, he has not replied. So, we are now faced with three months here in transit and must then rent something else furnished, short-term or unfurnished long-term. After several months of packing up, shipping off and hotel stays, we are pretty frazzled. So now what?

Today I met my friend Marjan, who helps company staff with their accommodation and was the one who found us our tenant when we left. Ian's contract in Kuala Lumpur was cut short by six months and we are back early through no fault of our own. I wanted to see if we could beg extenuating circumstances. Sure, the company is funding this transit place for us, but the other thing is that Sam, our oldest, has decided to move back to The Hague with us while he recalibrates. We need to help him make some decisions about his future. It's hard for young adults these days, with no job for life. It also appears that they are badly affected by the combined legacy of having had parents who appear 'married' to their work and having been told they could 'do anything' and needed to 'find their passion'. I realise this puts a huge amount of pressure on them. I wish there was a manual to help us know how to communicate with our adult children effectively and how to undo any wrong we may have inadvertently done.

Sam spent much of his childhood in the Netherlands and even went to university here, so it's a kind of home for him. But the company is not taking account of our adult children so the poor thing has to sleep in a child's bedroom and we have one room in which we sit, eat, work and live. It is on the 18th floor of a new tower block, bang next to the Central Station. There is a great view past the Malieveld green space over rooftops all the way to the North Sea. Everything feels too much to cope with right now, particularly in a tiny space with nowhere to put anything. Joshua, our 24-year-old, meanwhile, is temporarily in England writing a book for one of my clients on the local slate industry and staying with my parents. When he comes here, which is inevitable, the only place for him to sleep is the sofa!

In the Netherlands they make it easy for people to buy properties. Not only could we get a 110% mortgage when we bought our gorgeous flat above a shop in a cool street (the house we can't live in!) but they also give about 50% tax relief on the mortgage. This makes buying much more affordable than renting. Maybe half the price but here we are with no expat allowances and facing having to rent again. Worse still, the longer our shipment of furniture has to stay in storage the more that costs us too. I know... I'm rabbiting on. But it gives you an idea of what life is like in my head right now! Impotence hardly touches the way I feel.

I love Marjan. She is one of those perennially beautiful women. All blue eyes and natural pale blonde hair, neatly coiffed. She dresses in beige and cream and exudes calm and natural warmth. It was great to see her again. Dutch, divorced and once an expat herself, she is also a bit of a writer and we always have lots to talk about.

She cocked her head to one side and looked at me sadly. "I don't think we'll be lucky, Jo, at getting your tenant to leave early. Not if he does not want to," she said. "Unless you want to go through the courts."

I stared down at my *koffie,* took the round *stroopwafel* biscuit from the saucer and ate it whole.

The courts? That is not something I could squeeze onto my plate right now. I have a job to do as well, of course, but that is at the bottom of my list right now. However, Marjan is an angel in disguise. One of those people filled with love for others, for life, for the world, despite her own hardship. Her toddler son died while they were living abroad, her other child affected for life by the tragedy, and then she divorced. She has been back in Holland for 25 years, her daughter, an alcoholic, has never worked and lives in protected housing. But Marjan looked at me with those bright blue eyes and reached out her hand to mine.

"I will help you," she said.

"But we are on local status, we don't get an agent allocated to help us with our accommodation," I squeaked.

"Jo, I have a heart," she said. "I will help you as a friend. We will find some stupid house with stupid furniture and I will negotiate it for you so you can have a good summer. Get out of the transit place early. You can't live like that."

I lost count how many times I wanted to cry yesterday, but that was one of them. Later that day Marjan had arranged for me to take a look at two flats and will accompany me later this week.

How could I be feeling so sorry for myself after hearing Marjan's story? Life abroad can be tough and though Joshua had something of a breakdown back in London while we were in Kuala Lumpur and ended up coming to live with us, we did not lose a child. He's been in a bad way, been suffering from some kind of post-traumatic stress and lack of confidence and had more therapy sessions than I can count. But he is alive.

MONDAY MORNING EMAILS

When we were in Holland, Joshua, like so many youngsters, began smoking marijuana. I know it is a common rite-of-passage, but not everybody gets away with it unscathed. We watched him change. From a charming, sweet, communicative teenager, who received straight As in every subject, and who was in every sports team, to a mumbling, morose stranger who walked everywhere looking at the floor and then out to some party. He picked his university in five seconds flat by sticking a pin in a book, or at least that is how it seemed. He gave up cricket, then squash, then rugby. He dropped his bass guitar, the double bass, and the drums. At 17 he went to Thailand with two mates and came back with a Mohican haircut and tattoo. At 18 he went quieter and more rebellious still. Ian and I were worried but found it impossible to engage him in conversation. To be honest, we were scared; but his attitude was so antagonistic that we chose silence over confrontation. Not the best tactic, in hindsight.

Then, the summer before he went to university in London, he sat me down at the dining table in our lovely flat in The Hague – the one that has that tenant in it now – and spoke calmly.

"Mum, please can we sit down and talk? I need your attention, please."

And so I sat and he talked, and he talked, and he talked.

"I've been feeling terrible for six weeks, Mum. Really spaced out. I'm scared. I had an awful trip on LSD, it was honestly only the first time I'd taken it. I came over all paranoid and I haven't felt present since. I was with my friends. I just stared at myself in the mirror and felt like there's no one

"Often the result of an emotionally absent parent is a stronger alignment with peers, who might not be the greatest influence on the teen."

Becky Grappo

who understands me; no one who will remember me. I've lost all my best friends over the years, all my favourite sports and hobbies are gone. My friends now just aren't who I want to be. They just want to smoke and... I'm terrified. I feel that everything I love will be taken away from me. When I smoked weed again all the feelings came back. I haven't told my friends, and I'm scared to hang out with them again. What have I done? Will I feel like this forever?"

I listened as he told me that while his friends were getting into stronger and stronger drugs, MDMA and more, he had gone along with them until he tried LSD – doing anything he could to fit in. As a result, he had a terrifying experience that frightened the life out of him and he hadn't felt relaxed since. Like you do, he'd been looking this up on the Internet and, of course, had found awful stories of people whose lives had been ruined. He recognised that he had been blessed with a great mind and all the potential that went with it, but he was scared that these feelings may haunt him forever.

I was at a loss. All I wanted to do was protect him, reassure him and let him know we would support him through anything. Only a few weeks later, he was off to London, leaving us in Holland, and was scared stiff of what lay ahead. His experience with LSD had meant that he had forgotten to accept the university accommodation he had been allocated, so had no place to stay. It also meant that he had become fraught with worry anytime he saw alcohol or drugs. How was he going to cope at Freshers' Week when he couldn't even go for a pint?

It was a difficult two years as he struggled to connect with his classmates outside of university. He found solace in spoken word poetry and healing in the curative practice of Tai Chi, and decided he wanted to study Traditional Chinese Medicine. He made all the arrangements to quit university, and then he told us. We supported him, as usual. My parents had always let me make my own choices, though Ian's hadn't. We decided to let him follow his heart. But on the day of registration at his new college, he changed his mind and walked away. Four years plus of intense study was too daunting. He would not return to university at all. He did not want any help from us. He yearned to be independent, manly, and since he'd never had a proper job before, he wanted to experience 'real' life. He became a gardener and a labourer in London, while Ian and I moved off to Kuala Lumpur.

Slowly, he sold off all his remaining musical instruments to make ends meet. His poetry was going incredibly well, and he was surviving without our financial help. That boy can do anything he wants if he sets his mind to it. But as we moved thousands of miles and a seven or eight-hour time difference away, he drank too much coffee on the job one day and bang, the old strange feelings resurfaced. He'd lost his university friends by leaving. He was working long and hard hours. He had no mattress to sleep on in his cold room in a shared house in Tottenham – a bleak northern part of London. He suffered on the laminate floor without reaching out for help. He wrote a poem at the time that included the lines, "I slept on the cold hard floor because you didn't love me anymore".

One morning I awoke to 52 WhatsApps. A week later we went to London to rescue him.

Being so far away was hell on earth. We had to have him near us, and it meant that I had to almost single-handedly

"What happens if they move and become invisible? Who sees them? Knows their story? Are they able to connect and find new, fulfilling, healthy relationships? Often a difficult transition can be a trigger for a mental health issue like anxiety or depression."

Becky Grappo

pack his room and find a kind-hearted friend to let us camp out. He was agoraphobic. The local doctor referred him to The Priory, a very well-known private psychiatric hospital, to see a psychiatrist. By then Joshua had become scared that whatever he ingested would make him feel strange again. Now he drank no tea, no coffee and no alcohol. He panicked if he had sugar. He refused medication. He did not think the psychotherapists understood him. He was smart, he knew the holistic principles of Chinese Medicine, and he was convinced that though pills may make him feel better they wouldn't get to the root of the problem. It took six weeks for me to get him onto a flight to KL.

Eventually, there, he dived into meditation-based therapy and everything natural. The anger that was in him came out in a ruptured fashion. He was angry that we let him give up all his sports and passions. Angry that we let him drop out of university. It hurt. As a parent you think you're doing well, but your child can't always see your love. But Joshua did, thanks to Ian's suggestions, agree to get his place at university reinstated for the following September. Four months later he returned to London. I wasn't convinced he was ready yet; I felt sick.

He was much stronger now, but I was watching him from thousands of miles away.

He and Sam were living near Highgate Tube station, close to a high bridge over the road that is known as Suicide Bridge. It ominously peered down on his daily commute to university and, struggling with the new transition, he told me he'd been struck off-guard by troubling thoughts. He didn't want to do anything stupid, but he'd been living in near-constant fright for a year. How was I supposed to sleep? I would check WhatsApp and Facebook all day and night to see whether he had been active online recently. If he hadn't, I was ready to go and save him all over again.

By some miracle I remembered I knew a therapist who lived in the same road as him. Gloria, without doubt, saved his life. She agreed to be on call 24/7 and it was she who would lie with him all night when he was afraid, shaking, and she who would teach him about natural foods and juicing. She gave him techniques, based on CBT, and he filled notebook after notebook. He wrote himself healed. At the end of the year he graduated with a First. Now, three and a half years later, he has turned his life completely around. He was back.

In his final year at university, Joshua decided to take an open unit in Indonesian – being similar to Malay, should he ever come to visit – and ended up being entered into the International Malay Speech Competition. He got free flights to KL and won. $7,000. Straining to pick out words in this foreign tongue he'd picked up in less than a year, we watched him shake hands with the Prime Minister.

Following a yearlong language scholarship in Indonesia, Joshua interned with a rural biogas organisation. His boss believed in his writing so much that he sent him around the archipelago as a success-story writer. He returned to KL with a new career path and, under the caring hand of his Catholic father-figure in Indonesia, renewed faith in the Christianity of his childhood. Religion became his rock. Unlike Marjan's daughter, he has hope. Both our kids have hope, but they don't quite have what Ian and I call 'a safe place to fall', here with us, if they should want it.

We have lived abroad for almost 30 years; our kids were born overseas and feel they have no home. The only house we actually own, we bought after Sam left for university. We owned it for a very short time while it was under renovation and it is now tenanted as you know. I'm blowing it out of proportion, I know, but I want to be in our house again so much. I feel guilty that we cannot provide our boys with their own bedrooms right now, a place they can rely on to just be there. After our experience with Joshua I carry around more fear than is probably healthy.

When I saw Marjan yesterday she was smiling despite her own pain. She is writing her memoir based on her diaries and she told me that her own way through this mire was to seek out her own joy.

"I do enjoy life," she said. "I enjoy so much. It's important for me and it is important for my daughter."

This made me smile as I thought of you, Terry Anne, at FIGT this year and your Ignite session on how you too find joy despite a scattered family and mobile life.

With love to you, and good luck with your move back to Bangalore, back to Bruce and with your Matt in tow.

With love,

Jo

Monday, May 8, Kimberley, British Columbia, Canada

Dear Jo,

My heart breaks reading this, for you and for Marjan. It does not matter how old our children are, we always want to protect them. There isn't anything that prepares us to be parents. I have often reflected that when we hold our precious babies for the first time, we have no idea where the journey of parenthood will take us. Perhaps that's for the best. As we both know, the joy of raising children can be punctuated with trials to say the least. Your email conveys all too poignantly the difficult time you've had – that many of us have had.

I so appreciate the emotions you are dealing with. I know you well, have briefly met your sons, and as a mother, completely understand the difficult journey it has been. I also have compassion for your need to provide a more permanent home. And of course, on top of all that, you're in transition yourself after a move.

I stayed often in your welcoming home in Kuala Lumpur. Swam and luxuriated with you in the warm waters of its frangipani-dotted pool. We chatted and researched, and plotted our book, *The Pioneers of Penang*, about a place we both came to love. I'm sure there are days you miss it terribly. I also know we don't always get to choose when and where events that shape our life will place themselves. Is it the right time, the right country, a place with resources? I hope the housing issue sorts itself and you can build a nest for your family in your own home. Thankfully Marjan is embracing you with her wisdom and love – perhaps you are where you are meant to be, Jo.

Thankfully, a number of years ago, I was where I was meant to be when our family was thrown into pain and turmoil. Again, it was mental health. After six years in Houston, our family of five had dispersed as happens naturally when it's time for university or college. Except that in an expat family, it can mean a family suddenly scattered across the globe. We relocated to Norway with Andrew, our youngest son. Luke, our eldest, was off to University and our middle son, Matt, chose a boarding school in Canada to complete his last two years of high school. So Luke and Matt in their home country, a place neither of them had lived in.

Two years later, I will never forget Matt appearing on our back deck at our mountain home in British Columbia. It was nearing the end of the summer, not long before we would all return to our various locations or in Matt's case, begin the next phase of University. I was gardening, embracing the heat, relishing how great life was. Then suddenly, it truly wasn't.

"Mom, I need to talk. I don't think I can go on." What he meant was, 'I don't want to live.'

We talked, asked and probed. Had something happened at boarding school, perhaps abuse? Something on one of the

"There are many ways to receive attention and the word 'suicide' is not one. TAKE IT SERIOUSLY!"

Lesley Lewis

many teams he had played on? He was an athlete and a good student, not a great one but average. The answer was 'no'. He told us he just didn't know.

He (or did I and should I have?) changed his choice of university from the other side of the country to Calgary, close to grandparents and our family friends, closer to our 'home away from home.' Yet we were living in Norway when one of our sons needed us most. But this was often the case, support and help were needed for different kids in various countries.

Just before I had moved to Norway, I deposited Matt at boarding school, then flew off to the other side of the country to take Luke to university. No, it isn't like they portray in the movies, it's wrenching and draining. Yet Bruce and Andrew needed me as well in our new life in Stavanger. Andrew had started high school in a new country. A home had to be set up. A new life for me had to be forged, but that would wait. Is it not the golden rule of being an expat spouse: create your new 'nest', ensure your children are settled, and then you have a chance to think about yourself?

At the end of Matt's first year of university, a doctor had to be seen. Depression was given as the reason for low grades and pending failure. He was re-admitted with a doctor's note, an impassioned testimonial and a promise to 'keep things under control.' But at the end of year two, it all came crashing down. I knew I had to come home. Thankfully it coincided with the end of our four-year posting in Norway.

I rented a condo in Calgary as Bruce moved to Kazakhstan for a new assignment. He came back when he could or we rendezvoused in Europe – halfway and a place to reconnect. A night in Salzburg comes to mind when we felt we were on suicide watch. We hadn't heard from Matt for weeks. He hadn't answered our messages nor those from his brothers or his grandparents. He'd done this before. Despite not having seen my husband for a number of months, I questioned – how I could I justify traipsing off to Europe when we had a child coping with depression? When we finally received the phone call we had been desperate for, Matt was calling to ask us to bring a souvenir home from the local hockey team.

"We've been worried sick about you. You can't put us through the agony of not knowing if you're alright," I said, fighting back tears.

"I'm alright, you shouldn't worry about me," I think was his response. But as always he was pleased for us. "Have fun, Mom and Dad, I love you." Bruce and I collapsed into each other's arms and held tight. "He's alive, he's okay."

But he wasn't okay. Luke was on a gap year before his Master's and living with me at the time in Calgary – I don't know how I would have managed without him. Not only did I cry on his shoulder as I mourned Matt's descent into reclusiveness, I wondered what I was doing in my home country after 23 years overseas. Of course, it is where I was meant to be at that difficult time. Yet still, I felt my world had turned upside down.

Living close to the university where he wasn't really going to classes any longer, Matt chose to shun medication or counselling, and mostly hid away in his bedroom in a shabby student apartment. There were two roommates and

"Families living apart seem like a 'new normal' but we are only beginning to understand the long term effects of these chronic cycles of separation and loss on the children. Instead of assuming this lifestyle is an inevitable part of the expat experience, could we think radically and consider other options?"

Ruth Van Reken

a few friends, but soon they would mostly disappear from his life as he became more and more introverted. Like his friendships, his promise to the doctor to eat well and exercise to combat depression had fallen by the wayside.

At the height of it, his grandparents visited and wanted to see him. It was Easter. I pleaded, I begged. "You need to see family, Matt. You aren't helping yourself by locking yourself away."

My father asked where his grandson was and I had to admit that he wouldn't be joining us – he just couldn't bring himself to. Sitting at my dining table, I watched my father weep and his heart ache. He cried for me, for our family, and for his talented baseball-hockey-football-player grandson. He and my mother now understood how serious it was.

The next week, I resorted to threatening my 21-year-old. "I'm picking you up at 2pm. If you are not out of that apartment waiting for me, I will physically come and drag you out!" My son appeared and in that second, my heart broke a little more. My once exuberant, outgoing and active child stood before me, a shell of himself, like a blank book. As if someone had wiped clean all the love, the beautiful memories and the magical experiences. All those baseball games I fanatically cheered, scored, even coached... just gone. All those hockey games his father had driven him to while managing the team... didn't happen. All those incredible times sand duning, camping and boating while we lived in Oman. All the travelling and loving family times... all seemingly gone. Where was that go-getter who once glided across the ice as if he had been born on it? Where was that once gregarious, empathetic and well-spoken son? Where was he inside of his sturdy physique and handsome face? How I desperately wanted him back; the way he had been.

And how, just how could he be doing this to us when he had so much going for him? This unique and privileged life he and his brothers had grown up with, had none of it meant anything? Or was that the problem? There is no hometown. No life-long friends to call because they're scattered around the world. There is no touchstone. It all flashed before me. Yes, surely it was our fault because of this rootless, transient life we had given him.

But Matt was there, standing before me at the appointed time. Had he realised that he needed help? He had packed a bag. He was coming home.

Jo, I admit that Bruce has been far better at dealing with all of it than I have. He tries harder to understand anxiety and depression. I get frustrated and impatient, yet have spent countless hours counselling and supporting, crying and coaxing. And then, as I'm sure you'll appreciate, you question your parenting skills. The truth is, it is bigger than us. You know this with Joshua.

Matt is the only one of my three you haven't met. He'd be the one to gallantly hold the door for you, to make sure the doors are locked at night once everyone's in bed, the one to volunteer to pick us up if we'd enjoyed a night out. He's the one that becomes annoyed if I don't keep in touch when I'm out with friends. "Mom, where are you? It's getting late," he'll message.

And as one of my good friends has always maintained, "Matt is the one I'd want to rescue me in a fire. He's the one who would be your hero."

I don't know if I've told you, but the reason we felt we should buy a condo in Calgary, along with the house we already have, is so he'd have somewhere permanent to live. A healthy, clean environment, better for his well-being. By this time, university had turned to part-time, which turned into working for a landscaping company. Clearing snow in the winter, cutting grass in the summer. And so, you have no choice but to lower your expectations and most days you tell yourself that it's okay, especially when there seemed to be fewer 'bad days'. But still, no friends, no girlfriend, no clear direction for the future.

This past Christmas Matt told us he wanted to travel and come visit us in India where we've lived for the past year. He wants to 'figure things out' and promised to get the requisite shots and apply for a six-month visitor's visa.

"Matt, you're almost 24. You have to do this yourself, get your visa, and make the appointments for vaccinations. Prove you're committed to this." Months later, he still hadn't taken care of it. Fear, apathy and depression are a terrible combination.

When I arrived home this past month, Jo, after seeing you at the FIGT Conference, I was walking on air. My presentation about finding my passion and being joyous was well received and seemed to inspire people. Most days I think I've achieved that joy, as you say, despite a scattered family. As an empty nester there are but a few days where I'm not fulfilled and enjoying our life of travel and spontaneity. But when Matt picked me up at the Calgary airport after The Hague, that excitement and inspiration had to be tucked away. It was in his face, his demeanour, and his sombre voice.

"I'm not doing too well, Mom," he said as we pulled away from the airport. A few nights later, it all came tumbling out. We had gone shopping and out for a nice dinner. As the cityscape of Calgary twinkled through the condo windows, Matt confessed how much he missed us. Tears turned to sobs, "I'm so lonely, Mom, I can't live like this anymore." I held him in my arms and told him it was okay. He could come live with us in India. After all, he'd left the family home at 16. I felt guilt, sadness and despair to the pit of my stomach.

"I need to, Mom, I'm scared what will happen if I don't. And I want to go back to university, not here. Somewhere in Europe."

That evening's promises have at last turned into those long-awaited shots and a visa application. He has achieved it himself. Two things that seem so simple and perfunctory to most of us, have taken him almost a year to achieve.

"Mom, don't let me get to India and just sit around. I want to volunteer and I'll apply for universities."

I return to Bangalore next week and Matt will be with me if his visa is ready. If not, he'll travel on his own. He's been happy and working out again, a pleasure to be around. He seems at peace knowing there is a change on the horizon, a new chance at life.

In the meantime, there's a house and a condo to close up until August – a million details as per usual. And suitcases to pack for my 'other life' a few oceans away.

Bruce returned to India last week. We had a wonderful time visiting Luke and Andrew, in Vancouver and Victoria, but I leave them for another three or four months. And as is my reality… more memories, and more goodbyes.

Thank you for the 'good luck' with Matt in tow. I feel terribly guilty for having the slightest doubt about the upcoming change, yet I admit to you that I'm a little concerned. Bruce and I are used to jaunting off together on a whim for business or pleasure. We spend evenings discussing my research and work, playing Scrabble, just talking. We have not even bothered to buy a TV for our apartment in Bangalore. I have always maintained, "We're fine, as long as our children are well."

But one isn't and needs us; Matt is about to come 'home' again. It may be in India, but we'll make it his as well. Yes, wish me luck, Jo. And *sterkte* for you as well.

P.S.

I can't omit to mention, Jo, that I love the reference to pen pals and I'm so pleased we are reviving 'letter writing', though in a slightly more modern form. I have long loved this form of communication and wonderfully, my parents kept my letters and postcards I posted home from around the world. While I was backpacking at the end of the '80s, they would write back to me, care of Post Restante; so the general post office in Hong Kong or Bangkok, for example. Oh, how joyous it was to arrive in one of those cities and receive mail from faraway home. With no Internet, at least not for public use, and phone calls too expensive, letters were gladly written to and fro. And in fact, since that time, I have collected hotel stationery. It is now a glorious, thick pile of writing paper and envelopes – each one telling its own evocative story. Oh indeed, I'm so pleased we're embarking on this journey!

With love,

Terry Anne

Monday, May 15, Chez Vallée, Jonzac, Charente, France

Dear Terry Anne,

I write this time from France, where I have come away for a few days for a retreat with Sam. I was desperate for a break and it came at just the right time but more of this later.

Your letter moved me to tears. So Matt too has told you that he doesn't want to live. This is the hardest thing ever for a parent to hear. Why? Why? Why? Joshua explained it to us the other day. He had 18 months of constant therapy and worked on himself for hours a day. He's pretty much through the other side now though still suffers with painful feelings and anxiety once or twice a month. Anyway, all the self-work Joshua has done has left him pretty well read and experienced in the business of healing.

"Things are difficult. You suffer from anxious thoughts, you're wracked with pain and the future is not much brighter. You don't know how to find peace. You don't trust this world will ever give you peace. You want just a moment of respite, to find a solution. Death is the end of pain and, frankly, may be the only road you can see at that time," he explained via a recent Skype.

We know we should not discuss each brother with the other one. We know that it is wrong to lean on Sam for support and I was interested that you too leaned on Luke when you were suffering with Matt, and Luke was home. I guess we feel that the only people we can count on for their total support and love are close family members. When Joshua returned to university we insisted that he lived with Sam and gave him no choice. That was probably not fair, but we were clutching at straws and knew that if anything were to happen, blood would always be thicker than water. We know we should be strong, omnipotent, omniscient, infallible parents, but we are too broken and terrified to be able to play that role, so instead we treat our other kids as part of our support network.

You worry about your relationship with Bruce when Matt is living with you in India. You are right to! Ian and I are usually glad when Sam is out and we can crack open a bottle of wine and turn to Netflix, I can tell you. But then, Ian is so stressed out with a new job and its many demands as well as the hassle of having to focus on all the car-buying, registering with doctors and accommodation-finding, that adding the kids' issues to the mix puts him on a dangerously short fuse. We went out to Amsterdam on Saturday night to see old friends who have bought a top-floor apartment in De Pijp and it was a wonderful break.

Five years ago I had a burnout as you remember. It came just after the writing retreat in Tuscany that I led and where we met. I'd been building up to it all that week. Did I ever tell you that I was unable to sleep despite medication for the entire week? Now I know that insomnia is a sign of impending burnout, and is what a friend of mine calls 'brown-out', that time when a light bulb flickers before it goes 'pop' and extinguishes for good. I put my burnout down to a number of things. The first year of a completely empty nest, the second year of a massive renovation in the house while we were still living in it, and working too hard to escape my emotions. I have always buried myself in work, finding it the best way to stop thinking and worrying. I appreciate not everyone is like me, but for the first 20 years of my life abroad, work was my drug of choice!

When I had the burnout, it hit me that I simply could not think straight anymore. Twice in a week I had found myself driving on the wrong side of the road and only realised it when motorists honked their horns at me like crazy. I had found myself feeling dizzy and needed to hold onto Ian if we went for a walk. My head was buzzing. I felt as if I had stuck my fingers in a plug socket and was wired with electricity, fizzing with adrenaline and I felt not quite there, spaced out. The day I realised I was at the end of the road was the day I could not physically walk across a room. The reason I tell you this is that right now, I'm browning out. The fizzing is back. I am sleeping less and less. You know those kids' toys that you get in Christmas crackers, where you have some tiny ball bearings rolling about and you have to get them into the holes in the base? Well I feel that I have one of those inside my skull and I have to stand up straight and wobble the parts of brain back into place because they have lost their moorings. I know. I know. We've just moved. Sam is with us in a pokey flat and is a bit rudderless. He has a few old friends here but nothing like the independence nor the social life he craves. And he has no money. Now we are back in Europe my parents heave back into my mind and I feel compelled to compensate for being so far away for so long and am hiring a car and driving the 10 hours back to see them every few weeks.

I have coaching and counselling friends who keep on telling me to look after myself. In KL I did yoga twice a week and had massages once or twice a week (they were so cheap!). I also had an active social life. I knew I was looking after myself. Now that I'm back in The Hague, I realise I've not joined a yoga studio and massages are way too expensive to justify. Then I realised that I have not yet made the effort to reconnect with any of my friends in The Hague though I have been back here eight weeks. I lived here for nine years before our trip to Malaysia so I have tons of friends, yet I have not met one for coffee or a glass of wine. That same day I made appointments to see several and now that I have done so, it has been a boost. Mind you, finding myself inevitably moaning about all the stuff I have to do and to worry about probably makes me a bit of a pain in the butt to be around and they won't want to see me again in a hurry! Should I keep quiet when I see them? I'm such a sharer that it's hard not to tell all.

Anyway, the reason I tell you this is that you need to look after yourself too. I get out and walk every day. I read the paper, but you know, even as I write this I can feel another of the brown-out symptoms. It feels like someone is squeezing out my brain like a sponge. When I was recovering from my burnout I learned that cooking is a kind of meditation for me. So, I love to cook every day. Not least because Sam is here and I want to be sure we have healthy snacks to hand. I also learned that when my body displays the signs of brown-out, I need to take action and to take action now. I cannot afford another burnout. Back then the maximum I could sit at the computer was 10 minutes a day. After that I had to sit on the floor. It took me three months to be able to work an hour or so and six more to be able to work four hours a day. I still can't work beyond 5pm or I know I won't sleep. How I wish massages were as cheap here as they were in Malaysia. How I wish I could have one every week!

Our accommodation hunt continues. We really need a furnished place with three bedrooms for five months but it seems that short-term rentals cost more than long-term – furnished accommodation is even worse. It is really hard to find three-bed and furnished. Joshua is likely to live with us too at the end of the month. His UK job will end and as he will be unemployed while he waits for whatever happens next, he needs a place to stay. He wants to work for me, which is great, though I don't have that much for him at the moment.

I guess we'll have to go for unfurnished accommodation because we cannot afford the alternatives. We have seen a few places and those prepared to take short-term renters seem to only be happy to take us because no one else wants their flats! The stairs are frighteningly steep. We can't bear the thought of taking our own furniture apart to squeeze

"Take ownership of your symptoms: they are there to tell you something. Reach for a natural therapy first. Something as simple as a yoga or mediation class, a massage, using essential oils..."

Amanda Graham

it up the stairs and through the windows only to have to dismantle it all again five months later. So, we have currently decided to live with packing cases, borrowed and second-hand furniture in an unfurnished place. It's not ideal and at our time of life with the stresses we have, is a bit of a stretch but what can we do? I realise how much I'd taken our enormous living spaces in Kuala Lumpur for granted. There was room for everything and storage too, a place to do laundry, spare bedrooms and a swimming pool to cool down in both physically and metaphorically.

Marjan has been fantastic, digging out properties for us and she is proving a great support in more ways than one. Her wisdom about coping with her daughter is invaluable.

"I have to live my own life, Jo," she said. "It can't be all about my daughter. I have to find my own joy and beauty. And I do. I do. I enjoy so much, but it's tough. I have to be careful I don't enable my child. I can't afford to look after her and give her everything anymore and she knows that."

I look at Marjan, impeccably dressed, her eyes shining with fun; she is my inspiration. If she can find joy and enjoy life, then surely so can I. And I will.

Just before Sam and I left for France we signed for a temporary apartment. A colleague at Ian's work told him of a company we had never heard of and so I followed it up. At last! It is furnished, in a late 19th century canal house and though small, is very sweet. It's owned by a foundation that runs 70 apartments belonging to an established family and uses all the income from rent to refurbish the flats. Knowing how much you love history, Terry Anne, this would be right up your street! The foundation's offices are in the house opposite ours, date from the 17th century, have stone carved swags on the exterior and a knot garden behind. Painters Potter and Van Goyen lived in the street, as did the philosopher Spinoza. Apparently, the canal was once the city limit.

So, now we have bikes, temporary accommodation, are registered with the doctor, I've attended the company welcome morning, signed up for a historical canal tour and a workshop on productivity and have run my first talk. I even saved enough supermarket stamps from Albert Heijn to book a posh restaurant on their 'buy one get one free' deal. Oh, and the sun is shining today and it has reached 19 degrees. After eight weeks of hassle and so many trips to the bank with my passport, my bank card is finally activated and has a working PIN code.

It makes a change for me to feel a bit upbeat but today I actually do. We move on 1st June and I think it will feel like real life is starting at last.

You know, Terry Anne, when we ran that Empty Nest panel and forum at FIGT, I thought that we were onto something with this topic of the expat empty nest and parenting from afar. I knew this was a topic that, a bit like mental health, people weren't really talking about. But May is Mental Health Month, the BBC is running lots of stuff on the telly and radio and there's a lot more awareness of the topic. It seems to be coming out of the closet as a subject. Both of the boys inform us that the majority of their friends have mental health issues and many are on medication. Many dropped out of university or changed tack several times.

Few are launched into what I would think of as traditional careers. Lots are back living with their parents again, which is a body blow after all the independence of being a student. I guess that most of their friends have lived similar lives abroad so I am not sure if this is typical of expat children or all children these days. It's tough to be rootless and in limbo, but when parents, like us, have no home base for them, boy oh boy, does that add fuel to the fire. And boy, does it make me feel guilty! What have we done?

One of my counsellor friends emailed to remind me to take care of myself. Today she wrote in capital letters that I MUST GO OUTSIDE FOR AT LEAST TWO HOURS EVERY DAY. Studies say that going outside into nature is crucial soul food. I know that. Thank goodness The Hague has no shortage of parks.

Back in February I booked Sam and I onto this retreat. I was pretty sure he had a creative inside him and had seen a super event called *Head, Hands, Heart*, which would include painting, self-expression and time for reflection. I immediately wanted to take him as a treat, but in the end the dates did not work for him, and by then I had fallen in love with the idea of Praana Wellness in Charente and decided to go along anyway. They offered Ayurvedic food, therapy, yoga and massage, all among the vineyards. I'm a Francophile and Sam jumped up at it. Weirdly, despite the fact that he was my son and living with us, I felt I needed time alone with him in this kind of environment in order to get to know him a bit better – besides, he deserved a treat. He seemed to be rather rudderless and needed the opportunity to talk to someone outside the family, as we all do, I believe. Amanda, who runs Praana Wellness, is a counsellor who specialises in working with young adults and so it seemed the perfect choice of retreat.

Well, I write this from a glorious French house in the Charente region, where the shutters are sky blue. There are gently sloping vineyards all around and the off-road tracks between the vines and wheat look like ribbons of vanilla buttercream. It is heaven. The sun is out, the birds are singing and Sam and I are guests of Amanda Graham. Amanda has been nomadic like us, has two adult TCKs like us and has chosen to make a home for her family and a business for herself here in France while her husband works in the UAE (United Arab Emirates). A counsellor, Vedic practitioner and yoga teacher, she is passionate about helping people to heal and there cannot be a more perfect place for us to find a happy place within ourselves and for me, at last, to look after myself.

We have yoga first thing in the morning and last thing at night, called yoga nidra. We have booked massages daily with another expat who lives here, called Alice, and we eat sugar-free, mostly vegan, Ayurvedic food. Luckily there is also coffee and wine available! Yesterday Sam and Amanda went on a walk and talk, and today they are heading off with yoga mats on a journey in the countryside. I had a therapy session in the 'meditation garden' where she has her herb garden planted and there is a giant Buddha. There's a pool, a braai pit (she has lived in Africa) and a hexagonal yoga platform, where this morning we did our yoga practice and listened to the birdsong.

It is easy when we are embroiled in the emotions and practicalities of caring for our ATCKs and elderly parents not to look after ourselves properly. In my session yesterday

Amanda asked me about my self-care (it seems everyone asks this!) and frankly I am not doing enough. I am not doing yoga, choosing postures to increase the 'yin' I need and relaxing with meditations that help to balance my brain. I am not having reflexology and I'm not eating sugar-free food that is calming my pitta-vata temperament. Okay, so this may sound a bit wacky but I think that even if the practices are a bit unusual, my intention here is to look after myself and let Sam do the same and that is really important.

The sessions with Amanda are helpful and inspiring, the food is delicious – chia seed compotes with berries, flour-free crackers, Brie de Meaux and local Pineau as an aperitif. My attention is less focused on others and more drawn to myself and I realise how tense I have been. How strung out. How hard it is to sleep and how very, very tired I am. I see Sam in an environment that really suits him. The healthy food and yoga, the meditation, the countryside, the stimulating conversations and the attention he's getting from someone caring and outside the family. It's a privilege to be here. Getting away from the normal is a blessing and is helping me to take some distance from the mire of 'home', our transit flat and living on top of each other in a tiny space without our own possessions. Not only do I see what Sam enjoys to do, but I am also reminded of what I love too. The food, the me-time, the beauty, the countryside and the shared wisdom of savvy people.

In one of my own counselling sessions with Amanda I found myself in tears.

"And what do you want, Jo?" she asked. We were sitting outside in the open barn known as The Grange, lounging on wooden sofas littered with soft cushions.

My eyes began to prick with tears. I had not expected that. "I just want a house. A forever-house. I think I want to stop moving. I can't do it anymore." Yes, that was a shock!

I guess that among the list of things I needed to do for myself as part of my self-care, and was not doing, was therapy. So used to looking after everyone else, making sure they were well-fed, listened to and were safe, I had not realised I might need therapy too. Hmm. Those tears spoke volumes.

Earlier, during reflexology, I was told the hard skin on my heels indicated my mind was stuck somewhere, while the incredible flexibility in my feet showed that my body was desperate to move. The pains in my elbow and knee joints show that I am being inflexible. You know, Terry Anne, I am DESPERATE to understand my ATCKs, my husband, my parents and to be flexible and understanding.

But there I went again. Instead of having a head-massage for me from Amanda, I asked her to teach me how to do those massages so I could give them to other people. Does this not continue my pattern of caring for others before myself?

Amanda believes that good, balanced nutrition and a balanced life with self-care combined with acceptance of who we are, and gratitude for what we have are key. She believes many other things and I am learning so much here, I wish I could stay forever. One thing I know for sure though is that I must plug meditation, yoga, therapeutic foods, stimulating company, fresh air and self-care into my life going forward. In fact, I realise that I too can benefit from counselling. It is so good here to be able to think of myself for a change instead of everyone else. And it is lovely to be waited on, to be cared for.

It's hard to believe that in just a week so much has happened and that I have so much to share. I hope it does not sound like a string of mad ramblings.

In a separate email to me you shared that your brother-in-law, Bruce's brother, has passed away and again you have had to travel unexpectedly and at short notice. As if these weren't testing enough times as it is? I wish you all strength with the days that surround you and hope you manage to find time to look after yourself.

With love,

Jo

Monday, May 22, near Cardiff, Wales

Dear Jo,

When I received your last message, it resonated even more than it might have done a week ago. I write this from Wales;

I'm a shambles. A coffee shop is my refuge, having no choice but to step away for a few hours from the overwhelming task of arranging and hosting a funeral, and dispensing of the material goods of my brother-in-law's life… all in six days. After four days of exhausting work, I am mentally and physically fragile. My usual resolve eludes me this afternoon and I understand your description of a burnout. Yes, I can visualise one very easily.

Most people do not have the task of planning a funeral and clearing a house in such a short period of time. It's been endless and my brother-in-law was a collector, maybe the true extent of it speaks a little of hoarding. After packing up the 30th box of shoes, shirts, boots, trousers, many with the price tag on them (then hauled off to a charity shop), a certain numbness settles over you. It becomes difficult to be too emotional.

I wondered if he ever pondered who was going to sort it all? Why should it be left to his extremely busy brother, my husband, who has a demanding job and lives on a different continent? Why did anyone need 2,500 CDs, many unopened, many repeats? We understand that as a person who was declared legally blind, things could get messy and overlooked, but the sheer volume of 'things' is overwhelming. I'm sure this sounds cold and callous, and then I ask myself, 'Are any of us that different?' I have 'stuff' in three different properties around the globe, well make it four if you also count some bits and pieces at my parents'. Our family would likely be saying the same of us!

My brother-in-law was only 56 years old; complications from diabetes had grown worse over the past 10 years.

His passing was not a complete surprise and after a kidney transplant six years ago, Rod had lived longer than expected. But as Bruce's last immediate family member, his passing is a terrible blow for him.

As I was enjoying my last week in Canada, Bruce called with the news. Plans were made to divert to Wales instead of returning to India. I have now been away for more than two months and was eager to go back to the comfort of my apartment in Bangalore. Do some work, catch up with a life I don't really seem to have (as I'm rarely there), maybe just relax and be 'still'. After cleaning and closing up our house in British Columbia, I was on my way to Frankfurt as usual. Instead, I diverted to London to meet Bruce at Heathrow. He had left Canada before me; he had only just arrived back in India and then turned around.

I don't know how he's coping so well with the myriad details as we mourn our loss. "It's my duty," he tells me stoically.

It is and we couldn't have done it without the help of a few good friends and two of Rod's stepchildren. Their mother divorced him about five years ago and he had no choice but to forge a new life – it was just him and Neena, his guide dog. We had been there as often as we could for him, especially Bruce, but in reality, when you live globally, time with family is fractured and making time for your own children and your parents is foremost in your mind. We're here now and I think Rod would be pleased with the arrangements we've made.

We've planned two ceremonies for tomorrow, then a rushed delivery of his ashes to his favourite seaside restaurant, a farewell drink and a stroll to the water to scatter Rod's ashes. A chance to say a final farewell as we place white roses into the water, each saying a personal farewell. Despite the sadness, it will be an intimate gathering with close friends and family and I'm pleased for Bruce that two of his closest cousins will be here from Scotland. Especially as connections to his home country grow fewer and fewer.

Walking into Rod's house when we arrived was difficult – signs of life were all around. In his wee back garden a new cherry tree awaited planting, fresh bags of mulch were close by, and the parsley was abundant, ready for picking. That vignette really struck us and we didn't know what to do next. But we did what we thought best. We lit a candle, opened a bottle of red wine and put on one of his beloved CDs. We toasted to him and to the home that was – we toasted to its last day of completeness.

Now four days later, the exhaustion, the decision making and the physical exertion have rendered me spent. In three more days, I'll be on a plane again: this time I'm going 'home'. Matt will be on the flight with me from Frankfurt.

The blessing is that he has continued to arrange his move to India and is ready to travel. He is excited and as I write, he's at his grandparents spending a few days with family. It is such a relief – I feel I simply couldn't have coped with this if I had had to worry about him as well. There is only so much you can mentally deal with at one time.

As we both know, this expat life is a fine balance. The 'highs' can be wonderfully high, the lows compounded by distance from family, feeling detached and not rooted. And when you dismantle a life as we've done this week, it forces you to question your own life even more than you might usually. And perhaps for those who live globally, time seems ever more precious… there just doesn't seem to be enough of it. As children live their own lives, often in another country and visits home are never long enough, it is a fine balance between sacrifice and abundance. Of more memories created, but also of yet more unwanted goodbyes. And never does it strike you more than after losing a loved one.

Jo, you related your burnout in detail and it surely was difficult to write of. When we said our farewells after the life-changing writing retreat in Tuscany that you ran, and where we met five years ago, I could not have known you were on the verge of a breakdown. But then it doesn't always show on the surface, does it? It brought my own experience to mind, thankfully there has only been one. It wasn't long after Luke was born, our first child. We were living in The Netherlands, away from immediate family, yet I did have relatives a few hours away. I suffered an anxiety attack in the middle of the night. I knew something was terribly wrong and when it happened, it was a frightening experience. The *huisarts* was called and administered something to calm me and put me to sleep. But over the next few weeks, I felt as if I had been turned inside out and shaken upside down. It was as if everything had to find their way back to its spot, to normal.

I remember the doctor checking up on me a week or so later, sympathetic and asking if anything was wrong. Was I suffering from depression? Was everything okay with the relationship with my husband? He said something like, "Well it is not normal to have your first baby without family

"Does music, writing, walking, looking at the stars, volunteering give you the positive emotional health you need? Whatever gives you and feeds you, and supports you – know them, incorporate them into your daily life."

Lesley Lewis

close by." He felt sorry for me. In other words – why aren't you living in your own country during such a momentous time? I was doing the best I could and most days felt fine. I had a beautiful baby, our first home of our own, in a country I wanted to be living in. I don't know what brought it on.

That rawness is back as I sit in this café trying to find some serenity and calm. And as sad as Rod's death is, I worry about my husband. His job is demanding, often with travel throughout Asia. When he's in Bangalore, his commute is long, about two and a half hours a day. While I hide away in this coffee shop, Bruce is dealing with a multitude of things, including that of three overstuffed leather chairs and a sofa that nobody seems to want. We can't seem to even give them away! They languish in the small living room and I find it ironic. Everything else has been shunted away, that mundane 'stuff' and the must-have collectibles… given away or dropped off at charities. Things that took a lifetime to acquire and collect, gone in a heartbeat – sadly, as a life can be. I'm reminded of the fragility of life, perhaps the futility? Three cumbersome chairs holding on, representing what was a home. And once they do finally find a home, or their way to the dump, all that will be left are the memories, the good deeds, the anecdotes and the love. It is a stark reminder of truly how precious life is.

Your time with Sam at the retreat sounded idyllic and obviously it has not only provided some solace, but some well-needed reflection and pampering. And of the caring for ourselves… it isn't surprising that our bodies reveal our inner struggles and tell a story. Surely my tired, swollen eyes from the abundance of dog hair and dust, the aches from packing up a house, and the frowning curve of my mouth give it all away at the moment; I just want to cocoon myself. And yes, we need to be outside more. An image of kayaking in Norway keeps popping into my mind. As if it's screaming for the serenity and normality of those four years living there. I was outside regularly and felt I really belonged in my 'adopted' country. A place where almost daily, I walked along hilly verdant streets with the evocative fjord as their backdrop. A life that had structure and schedules. Where I had a job as a tour guide that I loved. A place that truly felt like home.

It's as if my memory muscle is asking… why am I not at yoga twice a week or at the gym regularly? Where are those long, exerting walks? Why is there no routine? The answer is that I'm on a plane about every three weeks and by the time I get back into a schedule, it's time to be somewhere else.

My inner-self nags with more questions. Why am I rotating the same clothes? Ah yes, I live much of the year out of a suitcase. Why, along with planning a funeral and packing up a house, have you been out every night with family and friends at the end of these endless days? Maybe try curling up with a book or getting some sleep. Why does one glass of wine turn into two or three? It's just been go, go, go for months on end.

As a neighbour in Canada asks almost every time I see him, "You guys are fricking machines. How do you do this year after year, all this travelling, live here, live there?" Of course, I always answer that it's fine, it's our life, we're used to it. Did we plan to still be living abroad all these years later? Not really, but we stayed on this path and once you're on it with one company, as you know, Jo, the tide moves you along with it. And most days I wouldn't change it, but the point is exactly what you brought up – life overseas demands that we take care of ourselves, mentally and physically, especially with so much travel and transition. I'll admit, it seems to be taking more of a toll on me than it used to.

And then family issues. Both of us know what it's like to have a child that has struggled or is still doing so. I have often told friends who have grown children who are working and settled, to be thankful… oh be very thankful indeed. "Do you know what a gift that is?" I've asked. Often, they seem to take it for granted.

Because we've also experienced difficult times with Andrew and I'll write of that another time, I feel a lot of compassion that both of your boys have had trying times. Let's hope your new home will provide a comforting base and that it will benefit all of you. You and Ian can hopefully find more time together, put the stress aside and start enjoying life in The Hague. I'll keep that in mind over the next few months as Matt settles in with us.

For now, I'm heading back to the hotel. I'll try to wedge some of this acquired 'stuff' into my suitcase. I'll prepare our clothes for the funeral tomorrow and try to rest.

We've managed to secure a bagpiper for the crematorium service. A piper always moves me to tears. Is it because my Bruce is originally Scottish? Or because a piper marched me up the aisle at our wedding? Or is it that the haunting, rousing strains of that instrument wangles its way into your soul and finds the most inner of emotions. There are a lot of those right now, Jo, and I'm sure tomorrow will be no different.

And thanks for reminding me… I really should take a walk along the waterfront for half-an-hour to clear my head. Wales is lovely with its abundance of hydrangeas and pastoral beauty, but soon I'll be off to carry on with my peripatetic life. Back to the rich experiences and the annoyances of India that I've learned to embrace – yes, who was the one just complaining!

Let's see what young Matt thinks of it all. I remember he once got anxious in a crowded shopping mall in Toronto, the crowds unnerved him. Did we mention to him that the population of Bangalore is about 12 million people?

One concern at a time. There's a 'celebration of life' tomorrow and strength that needs to be found to support Bruce. Good luck with everything and as I was given the other day by someone offering their condolences, I send a wee *cwtch*… that's a hug in Welsh!

Much love,

Terry Anne

Monday, May 29, Babylon Toren, The Hague, The Netherlands

My dear Terry Anne,

"A piper always moves me to tears."

When we are vulnerable and worn out and overwhelmed, many things move us to tears, don't they? Tears are probably near the surface anyway and certainly need an outlet, so let them come.

I saw your photos of the funeral on Facebook and it looked like a beautiful and poignant occasion. Reading your email made me really think... this peripatetic life of ours at this age and stage is bloody difficult. With close family members in different countries from each other we end up torn in so many directions.

Last week I was in England, again, for the third time in a month. It's 650 kilometres, takes me through four countries and under the English Channel and is an exhausting drive. I sat in my parents' garden with a morning coffee after reading half of your email. Just half of it and I was knocked sideways by the realisation that what we do is tough. That it gets tougher. In this sandwich generation we inhabit, we are

"The guilt, responsibility and obligation varies from family to family. Making the decision on how to handle 'ageing parents' needs to be discussed and the sooner the better rather than waiting for when it becomes an immediate situation."

Lesley Lewis

spread as thinly as a slice of processed Dutch cheese between slices of dark bread. Stretched to the limit. Contrary to popular mythology, expat life is no longer all about big salaries, chukkas and gin fizzes while our staff wait on us. I think that kind of life died out for most people before I was born.

Today, salaries are being cut. Postings like ours are cut short, leaving us in limbo waiting to get back into our own house. My parents are getting older and need me, besides I want to spend time with them. Ian's parents are in an even worse position, with his father now being a full-time caregiver to his mother, who is frail and forgetful at 93. But you are right about the wine. It's easier to have no wine at all than just one glass. Who would believe that this is our life now and looks likely to be so for a while yet? I too am living out of a suitcase for longer than expected – until November now – and I have had enough of recycling the same clothes, I can tell you.

It is only 10 days since I left that idyllic retreat in Charente. After yet another series of massive car-journeys I arrived back in The Hague with a stinking headache. Nothing would shift it. I felt sick and dizzy. The bliss of the retreat evaporated as I contemplated just two days squeezed into our flat before I was off again to England, this time to collect Joshua and bring him back to Holland, to see my parents, squeeze in some fab friends and see Becky (a wonderful friend whom we consider to be our surrogate daughter – she has spent so much time with us during the last 12 years) and Ben's new baby, Arthur, and attend Richard and Gloria's wedding. Richard was the drummer in the band Ian had played in when we were in The Hague before. The Reservoir

Dawgs was a welcome outlet for Ian, who has not managed to regain the magic of being in a band since.

Eventually, after five days, I tried acupuncture for my headache. Corinne, my acupuncturist, informed me that my headache was caused because I am 'wood', which I knew, and wood types like to keep growing and moving and when they are forced to stop and be patient they get headaches. Too right! I feel pollarded!

Sam is now working in the bar and kitchen of an art space in Rotterdam, mostly on the night shift, which is well paid if exhausting. He is happy to be earning. We are happy that he has something to do. He is also learning Dutch and has been accepted for an internship in an arts space in Berlin later this year. In order to self-fund he is applying for an Erasmus grant, given to young entrepreneurs who want to work internationally, so has to do a very complicated business plan. I am so happy he has something to get his teeth into, something that genuinely interests him and am thrilled that it is creative.

I shall keep this letter short this time, as I now have heaps of work to contend with on top of all the other 'bread' that sandwiches me!

Take care and good luck with the next leg of your journey.

Much love,

Jo

Monday, June 5, Bangalore, India

Dearest Jo,

I felt guilty for pouring my heart out in my last email, but your words 'vulnerable, worn-out and overwhelmed' certainly captured the sad week that was. Thank you for 'listening'. To a certain point, that is often the rhythm with this life. We feel guilty complaining about this 'bloody difficult' lifestyle because whether verbalised or not, retorts would go something like: someone else always has it worse, look how much you get to travel and the places you see, and of course, if you don't like it… don't do it.

Jo, as you and I both know, that is much easier said than done, especially when you've been an expat for more than 20 years as we both have; and we're not doing a U-turn anytime soon.

I remember so vividly being a new, young expat mother in Doha and meeting 'older' expat families. The ones with kids travelling about on their own and the moms often flitting back and forth between countries, just as we do now. For someone who thinks of herself as a novice interior decorator, I recall their homes with collections from their multiple postings. The few interesting Chinese cabinets and 'blue and white' porcelain, some Indian cushions and maybe a solid carved door or two. Those who had 'done Oman' would have the rustic Omani pots and the ubiquitous wooden flour mills that none of us one could seemingly leave without. And of course, there was always that 'must have' heap of Persian carpets. Both of us have acquired this assortment of goods which not only do we cherish, it's a reminder of where we've been; like battle scars earned.

Yet there's one other lingering thought I recall from those early days, my impression when meeting those seasoned expats. *You're still an expat after all this time? At what point do you go home to your own country and live close to family?* I remember thinking that it was a long time to live overseas.

They were about the age we are now, and like you I wonder. I wonder at times when I haven't stopped travelling for two months and then there's a family crisis. When your 21-year-old breaks down because he thinks you're only abroad to pay his university fees and he misses you. Or as you say, when you just want to spend more time with your ageing parents. And then when you know, as we do now, that our days in India are numbered. Where will it be next? You are right that the expat life is changing and as it's now June, there are a whole string of families leaving Bangalore for good, many because of the 'restructuring' of the company. I admit to not knowing the reference to 'chukkas' (got it now!) but I understood the big salaries. We both know those big salaries aren't that 'big' when you're travelling world-wide to see family, when there are homes and maybe cars in different countries, when our kids who are here and there might need our support. And 'gin fizzes', yes, it is no longer a given that you can live the expat life for as long as you wish or thought you might.

"This is why 'sacred objects' are so important. As we put familiar pictures on the wall, set up family photos on the dresser, or bring in the favorite couch from the moving van, life begins to feel more normal."

Ruth Van Reken

Driving back and forth to England as you've been doing, really struck a chord with me. I'm sure it's been exhausting and tedious; the only silver lining perhaps is that you're seeing your parents more than if you were still in KL. Jo, surely it isn't sustainable to keep this up as your headaches may be telling you. But as always, we do what we need to do. Yet on some level, consider yourself fortunate. You are in a beautiful, civilised city, surrounded by a multitude more at your doorstep in Europe. I emphasise this because you're not in a large, polluted city… let me back up a bit.

After more than two months away, it was fabulous last week to be back to that other 'home' in Bangalore. Back in my beautiful, modern apartment with its soft hues of blues, whites and greens – with its cool marble floors and lush mural of trees and coconut palms outside its large windows. It was a dream just to sit at my desk and finally write in one spot. I worked on my memoir, completed a heartfelt blog, just felt normal and relaxed again. And those suitcases finally got unpacked, no more 'rotating' for at least a month! And yes, I've been to the gym and to yoga.

Matt is here as you know and it's been a joy to have him, things are going well. He's getting out and about on his own, to the gym, lunch or shopping, a visit here and there with us to the city sites. Some family games, nice dinners, all of that. Yes, I am already missing some alone time with Bruce, but I won't complain about that. And in fact as I write this Monday morning, there truly should be nothing to worry about. We Skyped with Luke and Andrew on the weekend and they're doing well; working, camping, climbing, living a great life in beautiful British Columbia – both in loving relationships. Photos on Facebook show my parents with my brother and his family together on a weekend excursion. Somewhere close to our house in fact, so it was nice to see, though of course it would have been nice to have been there.

But we are in a city, which – other than my view, researching history to write about, some lovely serendipitous days in storied bazaars and the odd trip to a sparkling five-star hotel – can be a unique, challenging place to live. Seeing a place fresh through someone's eyes is always thought-provoking. Matt has done that for us.

The first week, Matt was surprised with the way we live. "Mom, last month I drove past a few of the houses back home where you grew up. You've done well for yourself, you guys have really achieved something," he says, roaming his eyes over the expansive apartment. When he comes back from the five-star hotel that is our club, he comments, "They treat you like royalty, almost over the top. Does it get tiring?" I give my head a shake; it seems completely normal to me.

And yesterday, after a week of being out and about in our area, we head to Bangalore Fort and Tipu Sultan's Summer Palace. They're not in one of the more well-to-do neighbourhoods where we live, but in one of the older *pets*. It is a soulful and interesting place, where many hard-working people live, but it's an area where some barely scrape by. We're stared at curiously, the only foreigners for miles. There are friendly hellos, but some are befuddled as to why we're there. I take photos of the fort and the palace, but put my camera away. It just doesn't feel right today. I already have so many photos of the countless vendors, the *wallahs* whom I am fond of. Many do well, but some sit under the baking sun, just a few limes to sell, maybe some gnarly-looking *brinjal* that surely no one will buy. Many vendors look too young to be doing this work and I know they won't be scrubbed clean, homework done, ready for school first thing Monday morning.

"Let's go home", Matt says. "I feel like I'm intruding. It doesn't feel right looking at their hardship." His sentiment has crossed my mind often.

We make our way back to our neighbourhood. Walking the last few blocks, we avoid the missing sidewalk pieces with their views to the gutter and pass a few aged, lovely villas under the shades of expansive rain trees. This was once the Cantonment area built by the British Raj and their troops. In fact, they say Winston Churchill has an unpaid bar bill just down the road at the iconic Bangalore Club, once the 'gentlemen's club' for the Raj. Since that time, from the '50s on, Bangalore was known as the 'garden city' for its abundant trees and ideal climate, sought after as a pensioner's paradise. The IT boom has changed things. Yes, there are still charming and interesting areas to the city, but the burgeoning population has put a tremendous strain on the roads and infrastructure.

Attempting to cross the busy street on faded crosswalk markings, Matt asks, "Has anyone ever stopped for you, Mom?" He too is alarmed by the haphazard driving and the lack of safe crossings for pedestrians.

"Yes," I answer, "twice." He's amused that I actually have an exact number for him. "I know," I add shaking my head, "it would be funny if it weren't so sad."

"Just like feelings of loss, powerlessness, or rootlessness that many TCKs experience, our feelings about wealth disparity are equally important to express to one another and grapple with together as a family."

Ellen Mahoney

Back in the apartment, our cocooned oasis, I wash the layers of dust off my face and sink into my planter's chair with one of your 'gin fizzes'. For us right now, it's still this privileged life. But is that not the question, how privileged is it?

We're all a little sombre. We relax and try to conjure our first trip away together.

"To the north, to Delhi. Or maybe the pink city of Jaipur?" someone offers.

"It's forty-some degrees, no thanks," Bruce says.

"Let's go to Kerala and stay on a houseboat," I suggest.

"The monsoon starts next week, not a good idea," Matt chimes in. I'm pleased to see he's been doing some reading.

"How about Pondicherry, where you took Luke when he was here," he adds.

"I refuse to almost die on that road again," says Bruce, shaking his head. He makes another suggestion. "Maybe way north, to Assam, near Nepal."

"But is it safe?" I ask, sounding cautious, maybe old?

"I just want to be back home, kayaking on the lake and breathing fresh mountain air," Bruce says with a sigh… the conversation peters out. Most years by this time we're just about to leave for home for a good part of the summer, but not this year. With me and Matt having just arrived, we won't be returning until August.

"No idea," I concede. "Let's just stay put. I kind of wanted a week or two before I started making travel plans again."

And so, as I write this, I have a quick chat with Matt and remind him that he should begin his search for some volunteering, he must keep his promise to be active and he needs to start researching universities. He agrees: "Absolutely, Mom, I'll get onto that." And he does but it's slow going, like watching paint dry.

And your news, Jo. I'm so pleased to hear that Sam is working in an environment that I'm sure will suit him. Now with Joshua with you as well, try to make the most of this time together, despite the small apartment, yet I know you need time for yourself and for you and Ian. I think Bruce and I will definitely be due for a 'date night' this weekend!

Thirty minutes later…

I've had to break. The sound of a thwack, thwack and massive thuds, turn out to be the din of a coconut harvester next-door. He has shimmied up the long trunk of one of the headmaster's trees and coconuts are now falling in waves of crashes and splats. With each fall, dogs bark, geese quack madly, and yet another tuk-tuk passes by. It's the first day back after a holiday at Bishop Cotton Boy's School. The cacophony of noise contrasts the serene view from my writing spot: the expanse of the rain tree, its delicate canopy reaching out like a grandmother's fine lace tablecloth, a nearby mango tree profuse with plumping mangoes, a cannon-ball tree dangling its odd, rock-hard 'fruit'.

Then I hear the cry of the *wallah*. It's Raj, my vegetable seller. I head downstairs with my repurposed basket from

Borneo and a few hundred rupees. It doesn't take much here to buy half a week's veggies.

"Madam, long time since," Raj says as he explains his absence last week and I relate mine for the past few months.

The usual crowd hovers about: the security guards, a few housekeepers from nearby, and a neighbour who strolls up in a vibrant sari and introduces herself. *How I would miss this*, I think to myself. *How will I ever live on a 'normal' street again without the colour, the bit of exotic, the unexpected?* "You're going to have to find a way," Bruce had reminded me last week. "We won't be doing our four years here as planned, it will be sooner."

The new lady around Raj's trusty vegetable cart is speaking. "I'm Ratna, but I'm from out of state," she clarifies. When I tell her where I'm from, her comment is telling. "So far from home and what of your family?" she asks with an ever so slight shake of her head.

I didn't need to be reminded, yet it is often the case in family-oriented India. When Matt arrived, the neighbourhood seemed genuinely delighted for us. Priya our housekeeper was also thrilled, especially when she realised how much he loves her cooking. I'm not sure if she can't pronounce his name or thinks it sounds silly, but she just calls him Baby.

Last week as she was prepping vegetables for her delicious curry, Priya realised she needed 'beans'.

"Baby, please go buy beans."

Matt grabbed a cloth shopping bag (for the most part, plastic is thankfully banned here) and walked the two blocks to the nearby grocery store. Asha's is no wider than a large broom closet, uses receipts tallied by hand, and I'm proud to say has on one occasion granted me credit. I'm officially a local! So Matt arrived back home with beans.

"No, Baby, the little green balls," Priya said in dismay, surveying the beans as if they were intruders.

"Oh, you mean peas! Priya, the little balls are peas."

"Oh yes, Baby, please go buy peas."

Without hesitation, Matt happily ventured back to Asha's for peas. That afternoon he also took notes as Priya cooked. You could see she was beaming with pride.

"Baby very good, Madam," she told me later. "He's a good boy."

He is. And the apartment feels more like a home with three people in it – like a family home.

I hope the past week has gone better for you and you've had some rest. And yes, I think our sharing is the right thing. I know it's re-opened my emotional writing. Of course, it isn't always easy to be so candid but I remind myself that after all, this is indeed our life.

Much love and a good week ahead!

Terry Anne

Monday, June 12, Babylon Toren, The Hague, The Netherlands

Dear Terry Anne,

A few things have happened since my last email. On June 1st, I went on a workshop. It was led by Blanca, a Mexican lady, whom I'd known from when we were here before. I knew she was good and so signed up for a workshop called *10X Your Productivity.* I came away inspired as anything and ready not to change anything drastically but to employ what she called 'micro-habits'. Tiny changes that feel pretty insignificant but make a big difference over time. They work a bit like Morning Pages (when you speedwrite for 10 minutes first thing every morning). You may not have an hour a day to commit to something new but you do have 10 minutes, or even one minute. So, from that day on I started 10 minutes of Morning Pages, 10 minutes of yoga and 10 minutes of meditation. Just 30 minutes a day seems manageable. To make this seem easier I am setting my alarm earlier and you know, it has been so helpful. I have slept much better, feel better in my body and am craving less sugar and cheese.

Blanca also made us set some goals for 2018 and so I am now committed to setting up and running four writing retreats next year. I have wanted to do this for years and years but

"Meditation is available anytime, anywhere and in any situation. It is my anchor, my strength, my resilience to life's challenges."

Amanda Graham

have kept on putting it off until we are more stable. I realise we may never be stable, may never own a house large enough to run as a retreat centre, like Amanda does in France. I simply cannot put it off any longer. Now, less than two weeks later and I am still doing the 30 minutes of micro-habits and have planned and put dates with the retreats. I feel buoyed up by this. I am doing something for myself 'despite it all'. I am excited about something 'despite it all'. I feel more alive and more motivated.

However, I do wonder whether part of my improved mood is down to having a very upbeat and motivated son with us. Joshua knows he wants to pursue a career as a writer and is dedicated and hard-working, using me as a mentor, which of course makes me feel good. I have enough work at the moment to be able to give him some editing work to do and that makes me feel useful.

A few days ago we got the keys to the other apartment. Desperate for some independence, Sam moved into it. In addition it cuts a chunk of time off his commute so makes perfect sense.

"I think this is the first time in three years that I have actually had my own room," he said, recalling the string of short-term sublets he had lived in during the previous two years in Berlin. This nomadic life of ours has robbed our two of a permanent bedroom, a place to go back to. I felt guilty, of course.

Joshua was supposed to go to the new flat as well but Sam's new job means he is rarely there in the evenings. Joshua can't see the point in spending lonely nights there so he is still on our sofa! He says he likes being woken up in the mornings by my husband making breakfast; he feels part of a family. It's amazing how two siblings can be so different. Sam is desperate to be independent and Joshua very happy to be at home with us oldies.

Instead, Sam and I met in Rotterdam last week to go to an art exhibition and so he could show me his workplace and meet his colleagues. They are all young and foreign. He's often in the kitchen and though he is worn out by his unsociable hours, he is busy and earning and with people who 'get' him, something I know expatriates of all ages talk about. We feel comfortable about people who 'get' us. I remember at one FIGT conference one of the speakers said, "Home is a place where you do not have to explain yourself". No one cares whether he makes a mistake nor how he is dressed. He's been lent a bike and is house-sitting for one of the girls next week. It was great to spend quality time with him too. And he came to lunch yesterday (Sunday) and stayed for a few hours.

Just a week ago, it was a bank holiday (how we miss Malaysia's 19 days off a year!) and the last one until Christmas. The Tong Tong Fair was on across the road on Malieveld. This is a Southeast Asian event with workshops, shows, music, stalls and food. Sam wanted to do a dance class and both the boys did kite-making. It was fairly silly and quite a lot of fun even though their classmates were mostly under 10! Then we found a tent of psychics. Sam was interested so, to cut a long story short, he met with an art psychic. After picking wax colours, she intuitively created a picture from them, using an iron. She tuned in to him and told him he was an artist, that he must be an artist and that he was standing in his own way, blocked. She told him he thinks too much and that he has a beautiful future.

As usual I overthink everything (I can see where both the boys get their overthinking from!) and when Sam was quiet later, my mind raced with assumptions. What was the problem? Did he not believe her? Was he cross with himself because he was blocked or because he didn't think he was? Was he scared that he'd have to follow through as an artist now, or angry with me for some reason? I usually think it must be my fault. It's often easier to blame myself. Of course, what I forget is that while Joshua shares everything with me, sometimes too much, Sam keeps his cards close to his chest. I was judging one son by what was normal for the other and normal for me. You can tell I am someone who shares everything too. Again, I wish there was a rule book and that my default position was not simply that if something seemed awry then it must be my fault.

One thing in particular that I have never felt confident about is my ability to listen. I am quick to confess that I prefer to talk than listen. I thought it would be useful to learn a bit more about how to do it, not just for my role in the family (though it may be too late!) but so that I can be helpful when my writing clients are stuck.

I learned the following and thought it might be useful to share it here:

1. Be present – actually look at them while they are talking, nod and make the right noises. These days it is too easy to be looking at a screen while in conversation, isn't it?

2. If they say something negative about something, repeat it back to them: *"I see. So, you always feel you have too much to do and it is impossible to find 10 minutes to write your Morning Pages?"*

3. Next you find something you agree with in what they have said and show you empathise: *"Your children wake so early in the morning and your day must be full on."*

4. Now you find a parallel in your own life or a perfectly good reason why they might think what they think: *"I used to find it hard to write when I had a young baby too."*

5. Lastly, you need to be honest and maybe a bit tough: *"If your baby sleeps for an hour after lunch why not do your writing then instead of in the morning?"*

I wish I had read about this when the kids were monosyllabic teenagers, I can tell you.

I still have plenty of opportunities to practice this with Joshua. He loves to sit me down and talk about whatever is on his mind. The legacy of his breakdown is still present and he worries about so much and lacks confidence.

While Sam goes out and about and sees friends, Joshua is more reluctant to do this because he is teetotal. He has old school friends here, just a few, and at 24 it is normal for them to meet in a pub. He is often nervous about it. He thinks he must be boring and will having nothing to say. I know I felt equally unconfident at his age, in fact I often had moments like that until I was 40. Joshua gets in a stew about this and his method of coping, unlike Sam, is to talk and talk and talk. One day last week, I stopped what I was doing twice, for an hour each time, to discuss one of his issues. Luckily he finds the conversations helpful. We spent hours discussing friendships and how to have a good time without alcohol, his fear of dying and his worries about which martial arts class to do.

In the end, after one of our long chats, he went out until 2am both Friday and Saturday nights and had fun. He really does need to get out more. So, we have Sam who likes his own space and wants to get away and Joshua who needs coercing to go out. I always remember the words of Robin Pascoe, who used to say that when we have ATCKs, 'one will want to go off and change the world and the other one will want to live in your basement.'

You can see why I need to carve out space for my micro-habits! I'm also determined to pander to my love of cooking despite being in a tiny kitchen, with such a narrow work surface that most of what I chop ends up on the soles of my feet. In the last month I've been making fermented foods. So that means kefir every day, a fermented tea called kombucha and I have started fermenting vegetables. I have been making homemade pizza dough, elderflower cordial and plan to make some jam this week.

It's hard having Joshua working at home with me all day too, because I feel guilty if I stop work to watch television or cook, like I normally would. It's what I like to do as a way of leaving my desk and recharging before the next bout of typing. I so like working on my own in isolation. I'm like Stephen King in that all I need is to 'stare at a wall.'

I so get what you said in your last email about needing two weeks off before you book more flights. That's how it is for me. This time I have four weeks between trips to the UK. I tell you, it's necessary. We still have no car. Cars, like everything, are so expensive here, so Ian has been researching and making spreadsheets as to the best, most economical option for us. Meanwhile I do the shopping on a bike, using the panniers. I've even got a pull-along Granny Trolley! Still, it gets me out of the flat and into the fresh air, which I love and love and love. The air is filled with the scent of lime flowers and horse chestnut blossom and that really is special. Yesterday, Joshua and I cycled in glorious sunshine to the Anglican church for a sung matins, then sat outside a café with a coffee before cramming our panniers with shopping for Sunday lunch. It really is a privilege to live in a place that offers such freedom for cyclists and when the wind is gentle and it's dry, there is little to beat it. I can understand how you feel in the heat and dust of India, that and the pollution that causes your allergies. Yes, it is exotic, and I have had my own experience of humidity, pollution and allergies from KL, and I'll take a European climate any day. I know how debilitating heat can be.

Which brings me onto church. My own family is churchgoing and for my uncle his Christian faith is the most important aspect of his life, his work and his personality. Ian too is from a family of churchgoers and though my parents attend most weeks, Ian and I are confirmed and the boys are baptised, we have lapsed into the high days and holidays breed of Christian. I blame the fact that we have moved so often and yet, in each country we have visited churches and attended the occasional service, but it has only been when we have lived in England that we have actually belonged to a church community, you know, involved in the Harvest Festival and suchlike. Nevertheless, I do consider myself a believer and so does Ian. I am ashamed that we have frankly been too lazy to go to church much at all, apart from weddings, funerals, family christenings and the Christmas Nine Lessons and Carols.

When I was in my early twenties I had a fridge magnet that read: 'Let Go and Let God'. It was in purple script on a white background. I still think of it often and take comfort in those words as I try to control or shape my environment and, in a way I admit, the destinies of those I love. Another saying I love is: 'Nothing makes God laugh more than people who plan the future'. Its irony is not lost on me for I am someone who loves to plan and dream and frequently build houses and arrange furniture in my mind in the wee hours of the morning. And yes, I do pray. It is the legacy of my all-girls' grammar school upbringing, morning assembly with hymns and prayers. I love the poetry, the rhythm and the comfort of familiar words. But no, I have never read the Bible.

As we move round the world I have lived among people of every faith, of Muslim in Dubai and Oman, of Hindus, Buddhists and Muslims in Malaysia and remain convinced in one thing – that God is 'good' with an o missing. I invented that phrase when I was at school and believe it to this day.

So why am I telling you this? Because, Terry Anne, you know, amid the mayhem of mobility community it is so important. And what community do I know I could trust? The church. And yet, doing so has felt too scary. I have not wanted to brand myself as a Christian. Maybe it's a conundrum of expatriatism; we want freedom, independence and yet yearn for belonging. I've not wanted to be 'out there', and no way would I ever brand myself as a Christian by attending Bible Study. But you know I love going to church. I love the music. I can feel the energy emanating from the congregation. I am soothed by the sermons and the repetition of familiar passages and I feel safe and loved and supported even by the strangers in the next pew.

Why is it that we often shun the very thing we know we love and need the most?

Joshua has climbed out of the pit of his anxiety with the aid of many things, among them grit and determination, but in the last year, thanks to his fast-growing faith. Our children are our greatest teachers and I know I cannot hide behind my fear of embarrassment when he is around. Instead, I go to church with him and love it. Joshua influenced me to join an Alpha class in KL to learn more about this faith to which I limply belong. Joshua led me to church in KL too, to the wonderful black and white timber-framed St Mary's Cathedral in Merdeka Square. It was my concern about him that allowed me to hold hands with TCK guru and ATCK missionary kid, Ruth Van Reken, when she came to visit, and let her pray for us. I can't tell you how excruciating that feels, yet how deeply moving and hopeful.

Faith is, I know, crucial to many expatriates. It is the one constant in a shifting storm of change and yet, until last year, I ran away from it. Now Joshua is in The Hague, and we have at last joined a local church, where they sing matins, have an amazing choir and, if we are lucky, the sun streams in through the stained glass windows.

"A community that shares a belief system in the deeper layers of our beings… one with others of many cultures and nationalities amid a sea of changing cultural norms in the larger world around us, offers a true sense of coming 'home'."

Ruth Van Reken

I think back to your FIGT ignite speech and realise that yes, 'despite it all' I am still capable of Finding Joy and that yes, I have so much more to learn.

Take care, until next week,

Jo

Monday, June 19, Hampi, Karnataka, India

Dear Jo,

I write this quite honestly, from the 'middle of nowhere' in Southern India, except that we are surrounded by 16th century ruins that rival those of Rome and Pompeii. Yes, we finally decided on a location and journeyed here overnight by train. After a wonderful weekend, we found ourselves back at the train station with no tickets. Contrary to Southern Indian Railway's 'confirmation', our sleeper tickets had disappeared. We could, however, buy a ticket to stand for nine hours or wait for the next available seats, five days away. So, we're now back at the small resort hotel plotting our escape.

The reflection of the swaying palm trees in the sparkling pool is my outlook. A sugarcane juice *wallah* just trotted past with a bundle of uncrushed canes and a cleaning lady breezed by in a crimson sari. Saris have a way of making even buckets and mops look glamorous. I adore the vivid hues of this every-day, yet elegant dress. I find myself observing them constantly. Yesterday was no different. As we visited one of the temples in the Hampi ruins, a refreshing, light monsoon rain cooled things off, "soft as jasmine petals," our guide commented lyrically. Against the pinkish-white tones of granite in the courtyard and temples, flows of saris drifted into the setting. Groups of ladies, one as beautiful as the next, and then families on outings to offer a *puja* at the temple. It seems I've become a family photographer as I was asked repeatedly to take photos of couples and families. I know many do not own a camera and they're delighted when I show them their image in my viewfinder.

"Do you have an e-mail address? I can send to you?" I asked. Most often the answer is no. They only wanted the occasion of standing proudly with their loved ones.

It was Father's Day yesterday and with the other two boys in Vancouver and Victoria, the three of us also stood together for a photo. Bruce and I then posed for our own photo in front of a temple, monkeys scampering behind us along its 17th century carvings. I love the image. We're grinning from ear to ear, barefooted and still in love. We have a multitude of these photos – taken around the world, starting from our first trip backpacking before we were married. That trip was meant to be for only two months, and yet here we still are. Still doing what we love: exploring, soaking up the architecture and history, and appreciating other cultures. This is what I adore about this expat life and why on most days, it feels worth it. Nowadays it is often just Bruce and me, but like you Jo, our children have also been romanced by this wonderful world. So on that day, even to have three of us posing at an ancient Indian monument was special and conjured family trips from the past. It brought back memories of when it was always the five of us. And when you are in those early years with your children, you feel as if that time will never end.

But it does, and I find it quite extraordinary that as parents we're able to adjust to our independent children as well as we do. I know it is our duty as parents to give our children roots, and then wings to fly… yet still. This empty-nest stage of life can be a difficult adjustment. For me Sundays are the worst. If we're travelling I'm fine. If we're in that other home somewhere around the world, it can be a lonely, heart-wrenching day.

We received lovely messages from Luke and Andrew yesterday. Andrew spent the weekend in his girlfriend Ayla's hometown, meeting her family and friends; embraced into another family circle. As happy as we are for him, it is an interesting adjustment when our grown children begin to spend time with other families. Is this more pronounced as expats, I wonder?

One of Bruce's concerns has always been that the longer we're away, could we become 'irrelevant' in their life? With this in mind, when we were home recently we visited them in Vancouver rather than only staying at our home base in Kimberley. We felt it was important to spend time in their environment and get to know Ayla and Trixie, Luke's girlfriend, better. This weekend I not only received updates and photos from all of them, but there was also a message from Ayla's mother. She wanted to tell me how wonderful it was to have them and how they already love Andrew. Another stepping stone in life, sharing your 'babies'. I recall one of my boys telling me, "Mom, it's different being with another family. It's nice, but I miss ours too."

I adore the fact that my guys often send me notes and updates, sometimes there are more from one than the other, so your reference to the different dynamic that each child offers rings true. I note the comparison of Sam's silence to Joshua's tendency to a more open nature, someone who communicates to work through issues. I remember times of having to 'walk on eggshells' around Matt when he was combative or dissolute when we lived in Houston. It was difficult and I often resented it. How could one person change the dynamics of a family to such an extent?

I mentioned that Matt went to Canada to boarding school when we moved to Norway. A few years prior to this, his attitude and difficult behaviour were often impacting on our family and we eventually asked him to sign a contract. We felt it was our last chance. It stated that if his attitude did not change, he was going to a boarding school, no choice. We told him we felt we had done all we could as parents. We were so concerned with the constant disruption in our family and that the other boys often had no choice but to be involved. As well, Bruce and I inevitably seemed to be pitted against each other. Your mention, Jo, of how families deal with issues when they live overseas is thought-provoking. Is it through faith, as you've beautifully opened up about? Is it by confiding in close friends, as I certainly did? Families are far away and it can be difficult to open up about these kinds of issues when you see them infrequently. Is it by trusting our instincts? I remember Luke in Grade 12, marching barefoot out the front door one night in Houston. Matt's turmoil and Bruce's and my fighting was tearing us apart; Luke had had enough.

I actually don't remember if we had been counselled to use the 'method' of a contract for accountability, I doubt it. In fact, I am aghast now that we went through years of family issues without any counselling or advice. Bruce was too proud, I didn't know where to start, and as far as Matt was concerned, he would have had to be dragged by wild horses. But I do believe that the contract played a part in finally instilling some accountability and improving his behaviour. When it came to moving to Norway, instead of insisting he went to boarding school, we gave him the choice. He chose to go to a boarding school in Canada, one that had a focus on sports. I have never admitted it, but at the time, part of me was relieved. I really didn't know how he'd adjust to a small International School and his relationship with his younger brother was combative. I confess I was pleased he chose to stay behind and I reveal this now with much difficulty. But I also had another child to think of and I thought about my marriage; there were fewer struggles when Matt was not in the middle of us. So aside from the joys, I definitely know the impact and strain that different children bring to a family. As parents, I don't think we're meant to admit this.

This weekend on Matt's first train journey in India, I looked at him a number of times and said a silent 'thank you'. He is engaged and friendly, the depression and social anxiety seems no longer there. He is a loving, confident young man at the moment. Can it only be two and half months

"Perfect families only exist in fiction. Real families have conflict. They struggle. They fight. But strong families, even with imperfect parents and imperfect kids, always come back to the table to keep working on that imperfect institution we call family life."

Becky Grappo

ago that he was in distress when I returned home? Jo, of course I'm scared it won't last. And yes, I realise this is not a normal situation… living the good life with your parents in an 'exotic' country. As well, part of me worries that this change has not happened through professional guidance or counselling, just our intuitive methods.

The method you shared in your last email is interesting and some of it seems common sense. I think we've all applied many of these instinctively, yet I applaud your openness and diligence in research and implementation. I confess to never having had counselling, except perhaps once as a child after a tragic event. Since then, I admit to being a stubborn half-Dutch woman; no counselling, have never been to a psychiatrist, have never been on Prozac or the like. Bruce is the same and baulks at even taking an Advil, never mind going to someone with family issues. Though he did a lot of reading these past few years to try to understand and help Matt.

So, as I still sit at the edge of the pool as we countdown the hours until a driver can transport us back to Bangalore, writing about Matt has forced yet more contemplation. My recommendation to anyone going through a difficult time with a child is two-fold. Try not to allow a child to compromise your marriage. You started together as two, that is your foundation. Make sure that remains strong and intact. Your marriage needs to still be standing after the often-trying times of raising your children.

Secondly, it's important not to compromise your own mental and physical health. It is essential to take time for yourself. Seek out guidance or counselling, lean on friends, get away

"Of course – there will be rough patches along the way, disagreements and more. Learn how to resolve conflict in a healthy way instead of the silence and the arguing. Be gentle, loving and true to yourself in your marital relationship."

Lesley Lewis

from the situation for a few days and most of all, find joy in something you love to do – and this also helps prepare you for the empty-nest stage. I found I often had to put that worry of our family away in a box, just give my mind a rest and a chance to focus on me, and my husband.

I finally returned to practicing yoga last week. I well and truly know its benefits and I know it helped me cope with those intense months of writing our book last year, just as I was transitioning to a new country. Without a doubt, it helped keep me sane!

It is in my plans to 'escape' to a yoga retreat while we live here and I met someone yesterday who offered a glimpse of that on a different level. We were wandering through a small historic town and chanced upon a craft shop. Noticing a tall rather gracious lady in the doorway, a European woman actually, we followed her into the shop. Its traditional whitewashed walls of mud and dung were thick and cooling. Beautiful banana-fibre baskets, bags and mats were on display throughout the once humble abode. But the real delight was Betina herself. She has lived in India for some 35 years.

"I've lived up on a hill, in a cave, on the mountain, had a yogi," she told us. "I found spiritually in different ways. And I was fucking beautiful," she said matter-of-factly. "I didn't find my life anywhere else; here I am."

She elaborated that society is too focused on beauty, on money – we need more spiritually. For me, it reinforced the difficulty that someone can have 'finding their life', deciding who they want to be, where and how they should achieve that. I thought of your boys trying to find their way and of my Matt and what our Andrew has gone through. I so hope they have all started a new chapter, one which will be filled with experiences, fulfilment and love.

On that note, Jo, I have to sign off, a driver has materialised. It's now six hours back to Bangalore by road. Road travel is the bane of my life in India; I simply hate how dangerous and nonchalant the drivers are. But no worries I'm always promised... most drivers have a small *Ganesh* on their dashboard for luck!

I'll let you know when we're home safe and sound.

Much love,

Terry Anne

Monday, June 26, Groenewegje,
The Hague, The Netherlands

Dear Terry Anne,

I write this from the third-floor sitting room of our tiny apartment overlooking the canal. It is a superb location for our street is known as Avenue Culinaire, yes, a French phrase in Holland. Here you will find the bars on barges and some of the finest restaurants. Once a year it is home to a jazz festival, where a shifting line-up of bands moor up and entertain for a long sunny (if we are lucky) weekend. The canal bisects two areas: the Turkish area, complete with its baklava, halal meats and hummus; Chinatown with dim sum and supermarkets that sell green mango and dried fish. It feels like home already.

A week since your email arrived and still I cannot get out of my mind the fact that you and I have similar lives, similar issues, similar heartache and yet we are handling things so very differently. There is no doubt that we are shaped by our experiences. They make us who we are, and they make us parent as we do.

My parents, still alive, at 81 and 89, have been marvellously open and tolerant parents, yet they too have shaped and added to my emotional baggage. My father is an only child and was adored. As such he has good self-esteem. My mother, a middle child, felt unloved by her mother, who died of cancer at 55 when my mother was just 18. As a result of his childhood my father is good at expressing love. My mother not. They never told my brother and I what to do, but instead let us make our own choices and then provided the utmost support in our endeavours.

When I was six or seven I was sexually abused by a neighbour. The police were involved and the experience was so traumatic that I blocked the memory for 12 years and completely forgot the most painful moments. My parents, so devastated by what had happened back then never mentioned it again, but aged 40, I went, at last, into therapy. In order to go to see the counsellor, I had to ask my parents to take care of the children. At the time, we were living in England for a few years and just a few miles from them, so for once, their support was a given.

"That fucking man!" my father said, red in the face as he paced across the room, pulling his shoulders up near his ears as the tension rose. And that was the last time it was mentioned. It was just too painful.

Ian is a middle child. His parents were always telling him what to do, what not to do, what to study, what to wear. His desires were rarely validated, though his parents provided music and sports lessons and encouraged their children to sail, to fish, to play in regional orchestras and to be accomplished all-rounders. Ian has no memory of being hugged and kissed. It was only after we had been married a few years that Ian told me about his childhood. He worried that he was not being a good father and, soon after me, entered therapy.

During the next decade we both entered therapy again. Ian from an approaching stress-induced burnout after a difficult merger at work coupled with the loss of our life savings in a bank crash. Me because, well, my earlier ten sessions at 40 had not cleared things up. I have a tendency towards a nobody-loves-me complex and needed to discuss the legacy of my own upbringing.

So, whenever anyone close to us has any issues, therapy has no stigma for us. Sam, who keeps his cards close to his chest, had some counselling at 17 when struggling with decision-making. He chose not to discuss what they talked about. to move widow line over the page back. Joshua would give me a blow-by-blow account of what he said, she said, and whatever he was now chewing over as a result.

"There are a host of reasons why people enter into counselling. In the end, the individual needs to ask 'self', do I need assistance… then proceed with receiving help."

Lesley Lewis

So, for us, therapy is something we know is out there. Because of my writing practice and my deep belief in the value of being authentic, I have learned much about the importance of sharing our stories as a way of bonding with others and establishing close relationships with my girlfriends. I also know from my research and experience that though writing about our own pain may feel narcissistic, in fact what happens is that the readers never judge us for what we share, or for being self-obsessed. Instead they see only how elements of our story resonate with them. Of course, were I to bang on about myself and to boast then that would be narcissistic, but I believe that if the stories I share might support, inspire or entertain others, then they stay. Anything self-indulgent goes.

So, I share. If readers find my earlier reference to sexual abuse icky or embarrassing or too much information they can skip it, but one reason I mention all the above few paragraphs of backstory is to try to find reasons for why Ian and I are like we are and why we have parented as we have. And why, of course, we may be responsible for whatever baggage and issues have accrued in the heads of our wonderful boys. It is easy to blame myself. I have demonstrated my mother's awkwardness with affection. I have backed off from the innocent, loving relationship I had enjoyed with my own father (sitting on his knee, for example, letting him stroke my arm while we watched telly) because I had sons and felt it might be inappropriate because of my abuse experience. Ian, having only ever shaken hands with his own father, had no idea whether it was okay for him to hug our boys. Such baggage, Terry Anne, and I share this because both the boys have accused us of being emotionally absent during their teenage years.

I am the first to admit that when the boys were bolshy and uncommunicative I hid my head in the sand and did not want to annoy them by prying, not realising that my attention was exactly what they did want. I was not a mind reader. I had never had a teenage falling-out with my parents and you know, I was scared of my own kids. Scared of conflict and confrontation and scared that I'd discover the reason they were difficult was because they hated being anywhere near me. Scared I'd find out that they really were doing the drugs I feared they were. In fact, Sam wasn't really, though Joshua certainly was and that was his downfall.

Ian has had difficulty making decisions because his parents were quick to tell him what he should and shouldn't do. I have no difficulty making decisions because my parents always let me make my own. Now Sam is hampered by decision-making and though he is excellent at applying for jobs and writes a darn good letter, he then finds it very hard to decide whether to accept or not. He usually decides against it. I wonder if it might simply be a fear of commitment but both boys appear to feel that any choice they make is forever and not simply a stepping stone in their river of life. Is it because Ian wasn't a role model and I probably just appear as impulsive rather than a good decision-maker who is happy to admit when I am wrong?

Who knows? Anyway, I think some backstory may be interesting here and may shed a little light on why Ian and I both feel we are inadequate parents and seek advice from others.

But what of the 'expat empty nest' (ha ha) since I last wrote…

Sam is still working in Rotterdam and is in charge of the kitchen alone today. He is enjoying it, happy to be making money and has made friends who he plans to move to share a flat with next month. It's taken a few weeks for him to share, but he has said that he can't put his life on hold, that the psychic artist he had seen at the Tong Tong fair had helped him decide he needed definitely to take up the Berlin opportunity. That psychic had told him it didn't matter what he chose to do because anything was a step in the right direction. It can be so hard for our kids to know what direction to take. We recently had a big discussion in the car about just this. Joshua was feeling fed up because though he is pitching lots of articles nothing is coming to fruition. He is looking at writing jobs and feels he has not got a chance of getting them without a Master's or journalism qualification. I think of myself and how I made it in that world perfectly well without any qualifications. Things are different now.

"So, what was it like for you, Mum, when you left uni?" he asked.

I told him how I had just taken any old job that came along because I wanted primarily to be able to have a roof over my head, food and a social life.

"I worked as a trainee manager in a wine bar in London but when that didn't work out I went back home and worked in a pub and applied for jobs, then when I got one in telesales I moved back to London. When I realised I didn't like that I got a job in recruitment."

"You mean you didn't aim for a writing job right away? But you wanted to be a writer!" he asked incredulously.

"I did apply for writing jobs but I didn't get them, probably because I aimed too high and had neither experience nor qualifications. I just wanted to have a job and earn my own money," I said.

And that was when I realised Abraham Maslow and his Hierarchy of Needs had a point here too. I shared the idea with Joshua.

"So, when you were my age you aimed for the bottom of the triangle while I am aiming straight for the top, for self-actualisation?" He was aghast.

"That's what all my friends are doing," Sam chimed in. "Living with their parents where they don't want to be and applying for jobs unsuccessfully."

"When really they should just get any old job because it will still lead them to where they are meant to go in the long run, won't it?" Joshua continued.

"Why hasn't anyone told us?!" they said.

I must admit I was pretty proud of this realisation!

Then, this past weekend, Ian and I went to England to stay with one set of good friends, to see my parents, deposit Joshua with them to finish the book project and to accept the invitation of other good friends to accompany them to Burghley Park for a Rolls-Royce day in their 1936 Rolls Royce. It was so good to be with old friends whose company was as comfy as a well-worn jumper. I'm glad we manage to maintain friendships and make an effort to do so. Yup, it was a 10-hour drive over there for just two nights and one and a half days! It strengthened my resolve that I cannot follow Ian round the world any longer. I have to stop and build my retreat business, to provide a permanent 'home' for the kids and to be more available to ageing parents. Ian's mother is undergoing tests to find out whether she has the start of dementia and it feels like our hearts pull us to the UK. So, after this current posting we are going to think differently. I need to establish something in England that might provide retirement income and Ian will commute to work if necessary. I am well known for changing my mind as often as I change my socks, but let's see if the resolve remains until the end of our emails.

I hope Matt continues to be the joy he is appearing to be. Tonight Sam will be at work, Joshua in the UK and Ian and I have a whole evening to ourselves!

With love,

Jo

Thursday, July 6, Jaipur, India

Namaste, dear Jo,

I write this from Jaipur – from the Rajasthan city of pink palaces, saffron-hued turbans, pretty peacocks and far

"Many of us will remain fit, healthy and actively engaged in life with vitality and zest for the whole twenty years or so and beyond. This next stage is therefore not the end of our life adventures, but a new beginning full of potential, possibilities and opportunities."

Nell Smith

too many monkeys. Sitting in an open-air lounge of a Maharajah's *haveli*, I am in my element. It is exquisite, with Moghul-inspired columns facing a tiled garden profuse with pomegranates. I have been bewitched by them since I arrived, these pomegranates. They are gorgeous shades of lemons and rust. They've been plucked and placed in small vases throughout the expansive *haveli*. They remind me of Tuscany, Jo, where you and I first met, where we first discovered how much we have in common. You are right in that we have many similarities and many of them run parallel with an expat life. Yet also similar to the lives of many parents, approaching or in the empty-nest stage, or even retirement.

It seems as if your decision of where to retire, rightly so, is now a constant concern to you. And I'm not surprised that some of what you mentioned in your last message is what we're also experiencing at the moment.

I've had some time for reflection on this trip. Perhaps it is this stunning setting of a royal family's 'townhouse' or perhaps because it is our anniversary and my 55th birthday.

I'm up early today. Jaipur is a city of astrologers and a few days ago at the city palace, I succumbed to a reading. It was the first time I'd done this but it was a better option than visiting the nearby Armoury Room that Bruce ventured off to!

"The sunrise and meditation are good for you," the astrologer proclaimed at the start of my reading. I am not a morning person, but I have decided to take heed. "You are Indian in your blood," he professed, "you like old and natural". As you well know, Jo, 'oldness and history' is in my soul.

"But think too much, but happy," the sage continued.

No, I don't really believe in astrologers, but he certainly seemed to get some things right.

I turned 55 a few days ago and I don't take happiness for granted. In fact, quite the opposite. When we've suffered a tragic event in our childhood as both you and I have, it is easy to contemplate other scenarios as to how our life could have transpired. I am so sorry you suffered abuse and especially at that age, truly sorry. I am not surprised that your emotions were suppressed and eventually had to surface. I understand this all too well and in fact at your writer's retreat, I was finally able to write about a traumatic event from my childhood. Yes, writing is therapy and because of it, I was finally able to give words to my past. I had long claimed it in my mind, but now it is in words.

When I was only 10, my mother almost died at the hands of my real father; medically, there is really no explanation as to how she survived. My mom had finally found the courage to leave the marriage and with her three children, all 10 and under, she was excited to be starting a new chapter in her life. At just 29, she had endured years of mental and physical abuse and was attempting to rebuild her life, but the night before Christmas Eve would change everything. As you remember, Jo, this is how I wrote of it in that beautiful setting in Tuscany. I still find it is the easiest way for me to share. It speaks to the power of writing. It affirms that our past is our past. It is who we are and by claiming such stories in words, a great sense of relief and healing takes place.

If you had known…

If you had known that your three young children would be tucked up in their grandparents' bed, not knowing. Not knowing if when they awoke, would they still have a mother… would you have done it?

That frosty night before Christmas Eve, presents wrapped, tinsel sparkling, warm pajamas on our backs. A mother thankful for a new beginning, secure from the dark memories of the past.

A living room that had just smiled with a festive family gathering, soon to be snuffed with an unspeakable act. Worst of all by a husband, a father.

If only you had known the heartache, the innocence lost, the emotional wreckage that was sailing our way… would you have done it?

The promise of Christmas had whispered us to sleep, a cacophony of screams soon jolted the calm night.

Her attempt to flee was pointless. The years of abuse now incidental. Three youngsters in the nearby bedroom, of little consequence.

If you had known the stigma, the teasing, the schoolyard fights your children would endure. 'Spare the sister,' she witnessed it… would you have done it?

Did you know your freckle-faced ten-year-old daughter was just behind you, running to protect her mother? Each gunshot piercing her fragile ears, each vivid snapshot more horrific than the last, each scream fainter than the one before. Would you have done it?

Would you have pulled that trigger?

If my mother's thoughts could have replaced her screams... Either I'll be dead or finally rid of this man. But my children! How can I expect to live as five bullets pierce my body as I shield myself – from my cheek to my neck, from my back to my finger?

I ask you now if you are the one wounded? The one without an anchor for that shipwreck you tried to moor upon us that cold December night. The one without that family you camped and played with, yet waged war with. The one without that daughter.

I'd like to tell you. Forty years later, my mother, that beautiful lady you almost took away from me had been under the warm Tuscan sun with a smile more radiant than it, itself.

Very much alive and vibrant. Her three grandsons splashed idly in the azure water alongside her; life's rich tapestry woven to this poignant moment. Her son and son-in-law were there too, and that once frightened daughter, now a confident, happy woman.

It has taken five years to find the courage to share this; there is trepidation yet I am at peace to do so. I love that I happened to write this at a retreat in Tuscany where just a few months earlier I had experienced that beautiful moment and by chance, in the same region. A moment when every pore of my being was full with gratitude as we celebrated my fiftieth birthday during a family holiday. I am now proud to own my story, my past, and most all, I declare how incredibly proud I am of my mother.

Jo, you've asked me how I've dealt with this? Except for the court proceedings that followed the shooting, for some reason I dealt with it mostly unfazed and rather maturely. When my birth father would pester us only a few years later by telephone, even after my mother had remarried (and in fact he had as well), a calm would come over me as I spoke to him. I simply agreed with whatever slander he was attempting to throw our way. "Don't go down to his level, Mom," I would say, hanging up the phone. To this day, she asks me how I knew to do that. I have no idea.

My mom, the lovely lady she is, never badmouthed nor judged. She got on with her life, just grateful to be alive and moving forward. She married my dad, the man I claimed immediately as my dad. When a phone call came from my birth father not long after I was in college and had moved to the 'big city', I told him he had given up the right to be my father. I reminded him that three young children had almost not had a mother, that there was no relationship between us. For the most part, that's been how I've personally faced it – rather matter-of-factly. And of course, every December 23rd, I say a silent prayer… *thank you, thank you for my mother.*

Like all of us, the past shapes who we are today. Even now I cannot bear to see a gun up close or watch an overtly violent movie, period! I get extremely emotional, as does my mom, when there's yet another mass shooting in the US, for example. And I expect that you and I are more wired to be

"When you choose
to see career from a
holistic perspective,
as part of your 'ikigai',
then many more
possibilities appear
to find fulfillment.
Volunteering is a
valuable way to use
and develop your skills
to achieve results
that are personally
meaningful to you."

Colleen Reichrath-Smith

sensitive to others' pain because of what happened to us in our childhoods.

While we lived in Houston I decided to volunteer. I had taught ESL in various countries and because of my visa, was suddenly unable to work. A volunteer role presented itself – counselling high-school students at risk because of violence and issues at home. One of the girls I saw weekly for two years, admits to graduating only because she had me to speak to, to confide in, to be there for her when she wanted to give up. She knew my story. "Look at my life," I would tell her, "I never thought I would have this blessed life. I was lucky, my mom is still here. I'm here with you because I got another chance." I would tell her that you can direct your life despite trials and sadness. That you can succeed when it feels you won't. That I truly cared… that I truly felt I was meant to be there for her. It is one of the most rewarding things I've ever done. She has just thanked me again recently and told me she loves me forever. I told her that I too, love her forever.

It seems part of me is very resilient because of my childhood and I see things differently with my own children. I admit to only having so much patience with 'supposed hardships.' The day I finally told Luke and Matt of my childhood (Andrew was still too young), we had gone shopping and they were complaining about some inane thing. I snapped. Marching them into the house, I sat them on the stairs and told them what true heartache was. How dare they take for granted what they had. How dare they not be thankful. I had always wondered when the 'right' time would be to tell them. I didn't choose it, instead it chose the time – like a living thing. The story came tumbling out.

Perhaps this also partly explains why my mother and I are so close. We've suffered, endured, but have also lived and experienced so many rich, beautiful moments. She and my dad have travelled the world with us and enjoyed experiences they would not have had if we weren't living this global life. Together we've hiked the mountains of Oman, scoured the souks of Qatar, cruised the fjords of Norway and melted at a 'million' baseball games in the heat of Texas. They've supported our life whole-heartedly. Yet they also understand the challenges of it; that it isn't always as glamorous as it appears. My Dutch-born mother and I also have an added bond because of my ties with The Netherlands – where I've lived and where our Luke was born. There were five generations alive when he was born. My grandmother and mother were lauded as a successful immigrant story.

"My childhood ended at 10," my mom contends. That was her age when she and her family sailed to Canada, leaving a middle-class life behind. Between the six family members, they knew one word of English, well two… Coca-Cola. Her father uprooted four young children for a better life, which he later achieved in a window and door business. Yet not before some years of toil and difficult times enduring work 'beneath them', sugar beet hoeing and asparagus picking. But despite the hardship, they were proud to be starting a new life in Canada. My mother was placed into first grade at 10 years of age, yet occasionally taken out of school to work in the fields. When the children returned home from school each day, my stoic grandparents insisted that they teach them: "What words did you learn today?"

They knew that to succeed they had to learn English, and initially very little Dutch was spoken at home. There were days when my grandmother had a difficult time raising her children. She dealt with immigrant racism and for a time, a 'home' that was the attic of a machine shop; snow drifting through the roof, the odd rat scurrying about. How utterly distant the tidy, quaint cobblestoned streets of Holland must have seemed. But Margje had great fortitude, the women in our family generally do. And there can be a no-nonsense attitude. When my mother became pregnant with me at 18, she was told she wouldn't be returning back home. "You've made your bed, you'll have to lie in it."

You mention having been accused of being 'emotionally absent' as a mother, Jo. This is understandable when we deal with our own past as we raise children the best we can. We're all a product of our childhood and our cultural roots. I think the older we get, we realise that our parents have done the best they could with the background and tools they had. Just as we attempt to do the same.

I read with empathy when you described Ian's childhood and how it has shaped him, and hence your family. Conversely, Bruce had a rather idyllic childhood in Scotland with loving parents. Their house was on the edge of the woods where they played endlessly with cousins and friends; a beautiful place where the trees had names like Thunderbird and Big Ben. From the age of 11, Bruce travelled the world swimming for Team Scotland, he excelled at school, he was well loved – the town's 'golden boy' in many respects. We had very different childhoods. Yet we both had love, opportunities, and a strong foundation with loving, extended families.

I think we've not done too badly with our three sons as they reassure us often. In fact, I remember Andrew saying,

"I haven't really suffered or been tested in any way." That certainly changed a few years ago and I'll wait for his upcoming birthday to write of that. As I read about your two and how they're moving forward, I have thought often of Joshua's story since reading it. It is clear to see how hard-earned a happy life can be for some. How easy a life can spiral off its axis because of myriad issues. And then when we question how our parenting has influenced their lives, it can be a confusing and hurtful place.

The truthfulness of yours and Ian's family life is poignant. We all know as parents we only get one chance and what if indeed we've gotten it wrong or could have done things differently? We all question it... surely every parent does? Even though we've both related the past lately, in our family right now, we are concerned for the future. Yet again it seems we are on the same page, Jo. What are we doing about the future and more pointedly, are we directing it instead of just flowing with the tide?

On the evening of our anniversary here in Jaipur, Matt did the gentlemanly thing and insisted Bruce and I dine alone. The restaurant at the Samode Haveli is a dreamy setting and I admit to being entirely pleased it was just the two of us. Things are going well now Matt is with us. Still, I wanted some time alone with my husband on our 27th anniversary.

What transpired through the evening was Bruce's revelation, and insistence, that he is trying to make a career change so we can go home to Canada. Like you are beginning to realise, he wants to be home. Period. He wants a life there before we retire, to ease further into our community while we are working and not retirees. He wants to be home so our adult children can visit more often than they're able to now.

"We'll still travel," he promises, "but I hope India is the final chapter in our overseas career. Ter, nine countries sounds like a good number to call it quits, don't you think?"

We continue the conversation with a nightcap in the open lounge, the call of cicadas and the light of the moon our only company. As usual I am ambivalent when it comes to the subject of living in Canada permanently. I have written of this, but this was a different conversation.

After going back and forth about the pros and cons of leaving an expat life, Bruce has had enough. "Honey, what do you want? It's time we make a decision."

I look around at the grandeur I'm sitting in, like a setting from a movie, one that all expats find themselves in. Settings that you couldn't truly describe to someone who hasn't experienced them. One that I completely embrace and cherish, for this is one of the reasons we live this expat life. Because we get to see and do the enchanted. And I use this word purposefully… enchanted settings and experiences.

Once again, I give this as my defence for not knowing if I can go home. I've said it often. "Bruce, how can I give up this life? Yes there are tough times, but look around you, honey, this is what I love."

But no, my husband is no longer enticed by liveried waiters, exotic hotels and wanderlust adventures. "I've had enough. I want my own country."

When I protest, he points out, "We want two different things, then. And honestly, how can you want to stay away even longer, from our children, from your parents?"

It sounds harsh, even hurtful, yet it's true. My boys know I am reluctant to come home. They know this mother they love has an issue with being in one place for more than a month or two. She can't resist exploring. She is afraid of repatriating.

The fear of being 'like everyone else' and not unique. The fear of stagnating, of not being inspired, of not being the one who gets to jet off. What had Matt written on my birthday card? *Your youthful exuberance is surely unrivalled for a woman of 55 years young. And we love you dearly for that...*

He is partly referring to my zest for travelling. He commented yesterday that we don't stop, how we can wander and explore for hours on end? How can I pause to talk to so many people?

Bruce interrupts my thoughts. "It's time you plan your future around being home, hon. You could lecture on cruise ships, go off on writing assignments, give writing retreats," he says lovingly, but pointedly. And he's right, I've done some of this and it is part of my plan going forward.

I pick up one of the golden pomegranates from a crystal bowl. I feel the rough texture, its skin reaching to its crown-like pointed top, suggesting the rather exotic fruit inside. I tell myself that my love for travel, for beauty and elegance especially in unique settings, doesn't have to end when I'm

"We wonder, 'if travelling seems such a part of who I am, who will I be if I stop moving? Will I still be me?' This is a critical time in life to double check our basic sense of identity and to continue discovering what it means to be 'me'."

Ruth Van Reken

no longer an expat. I think of all the parts that conjoin to make this one fruit – I'll have to add another dimension, a new chapter to my one life. And it occurs to me that I also have to do this for my husband. His hard work has given us the gift of living a global life and now he desperately wants to live in his adopted country, his home of Canada.

I think of my family and I know he's right. Jo, as you now have the need for a forever-home, I wish my desire for that was as strong. I admit I will have to work towards it, set some goals, change my mindset.

I remember something else the astrologer said, again I don't believe in them... yet still. He mentioned I should be training. That I will take to mean to go forward with workshops and more retreats, perhaps speaking.

And he said, "Good life, good marriage." That I'll interpret as joining Bruce in his dream – and also to make it mine perhaps a little sooner than I anticipated.

Lastly the sage said something a bit quirky, but for someone whose favourite colour is white, I rather liked it. "Always wear white on Monday."

So from here on hence, while I write my Monday Morning Emails, I shall be wearing white. A reminder to prepare myself for the next chapter, to be mindful of it.

As the evening draws to a close, I re-read the words on my birthday card from Bruce. Not able to find a proper birthday card in Jaipur, it is actually a rather large postcard of the stunning 'Palace of the Winds'. We stood before its nine-hundred-and-fifty-some latticed windows when we were here in 1989.

Where has the time gone, it's now 2017, and joyously we've shared another adventure.

Jaipur, 1st July 2017… Happy Birthday Terry Anne! All those years ago, we would have never have imagined that our journey together would have taken us this far and into so many corners of the globe. Nor that it would have been so fruitful and rich, filled with the joy of raising sons, the excitement of new cultures and the growth of our enduring love. Thank you for being my travel partner for nearly 29 years, my wife of 27 – my past, my present and my future….

I surreptitiously pluck some pomegranates to stuff into my suitcase. I'll place them on my desk once I'm home; they'll remind me of my promise to move forward...

Love,

Terry Anne

Thursday, July 13, Groenewegje, The Hague, The Netherlands

Dear Terry Anne,

Much of your email has stayed with me in the days since I received it. It's amazing how much I noticed its absence when it was a few days late, as you too noticed the absence of mine this week. Like you, I had an excuse, and though mine was not as exotic as Jaipur it was no less glorious.

Oh my goodness, Terry Anne. Your story, your openness, your vulnerability, your honesty. I am blown away by your last email. It is not surprising it has stayed with me. Of course, I knew the majority of what I think of as 'your story' but your ability to share it is exemplary. I wonder how it felt to write it? Okay, I know it was tough and took a hell of a lot of guts. I expect it made you cry too, but then they say if you don't feel emotional when you write, the reader won't feel that emotion either when they read. You were very, very brave. I wonder how therapeutic you have found writing it down here as well. Of course, this is 'your story' and as such has shaped you and affected not only your life but your family's too. Our letters have revealed so much more of who you really are and now I think I understand a little of why you seem so strong, so resilient despite your awful, terrifying experience.

It is clear that despite this you have risen above it and gone on to create a happy, loving family. That alone is a major achievement. Not many could do this, but then maybe it is that Dutch blood in your veins, the robust nature of your immigrant mother and even the fact that you clearly married the right man, that are responsible?

And those pomegranates! Despite the harrowing content of your email you still wrote me a story, framed by the metaphor of a fruit that looks relatively unexciting on the outside but is studded with a jewellery box of sweet rubies within. It feels wrong to change the subject and move on with what's been happening in my life, but I must. These emails are all about sharing secrets and baring souls. My friend Geraldine believes that our old friends are made special because they 'hold our stories for us'. Thank you for letting me 'hold your story'. Now I must change the subject after all.

Anne was my closest friend when we lived in KL though her stay was cut short to just two years before she headed back from whence she came, this time empty-nested – to Dubai. In February, I went to stay with her there and now it was her turn to come to me. The weather was kind and I was delighted to have a playmate for a few days, even if it did mean turfing Sam out of his room so she could have one that did not entail climbing a ladder up to beneath the eaves.

We had a glorious few days. Bikes the first day, through the city, skirting woods to the beach, along the shiny new promenade to the beach bar where we celebrated our 50ths six years ago, then home via a lunch stop in the Archipelbuurt in the garden of the café next door to the house we can't return to… yet! Hold that thought.

We decided on a 'favourite things in Holland' theme for dinner that night and I had a ball revisiting the shops on my street for raw herring from Zee op Tafel, rice and sesame bread from Kruidentuin (getting a massive welcome home hug from Anton when I went in), Saltufo salami with truffle from Gransjean the best deli in the Netherlands, asparagus and aubergine from the stall outside the ATM. A favourite things meal is never a favourite things meal without *muttabl*, a smoked aubergine and tahini dip, Ian's number one choice, reminding us of days in the Middle East. The joy I felt not only from introducing 'my place' to Anne but also from purchasing a selection of foods that make my heart sing, was off the scale. In this life of constant upheaval, multiple arrivals and departures and too many months of being a rookie newbie, a feeling of belonging is worth celebrating, don't you think?

As you wrote a week or so ago, it is always revealing to see our towns through the eyes of a visitor we are showing around – in your case Matt, in mine, Anne. For me, this helped me to appreciate where I am more fully. With Anne I have rejoiced in the majesty of The Hague, its amazing architecture, its safe cycle lanes, its greenness, its cobbled bits and winding bits and have felt proud when Anne has been entranced by the place. To hear her say she wished she could live here was the greatest tonic. We've cycled The Hague, trammed it to Delft to the pottery and the old town, visited the Vermeer museum, visited the Mauritshuis in The Hague and how chuffed I felt when Anne declared how wonderful she found the art. Who knew? In KL I had no idea of her hidden depths. It was a place without endless streets of fine architecture, no golden age of art and no cobbles. I also introduced her to *bitterballen, kroket, stroopwafelen* and *pannekoek*. Not very healthy, the Dutch cuisine!

You dropped your 'going home' bombshell just as I welcomed Anne. I empathise whole-heartedly when you admit to adoring your expat lifestyle. I love the ability to take a Maharajah lifestyle for granted (not now we are on a local status posting mind you, but we've had our 'Club Med' postings). I love the excitement of living somewhere so cool that friends visit. I love being a tour guide. Oh, gosh, Terry Anne, you and I have so much in common too! I hear you. I hear you. I'd only go home if I knew I could travel and you know that is exactly why I plan to run my retreats, do cruise ships and make my work fund my travel habit. I've done this for years. It's how I survived every 'normal' period of our lives when we had no company travel budget. It works for me. I'd simply go stay with a friend in a place, organise workshops that would fund my flight and enough spendypennies for me to have a free holiday for a few days and go home with a bit of cash in my pocket. Fortunately, I have spent the last decades building a huge database of people who have been on my workshops elsewhere and can now go back to them to tell them about my retreats. My Me-Treats. All planned and advertised on my websites now. This is my repatriation planning!

And so, I return to the subject of our house. Amazingly, 10 days ago on the last working day of June we got word that our tenant had gone! He gave us no warning. Sure, he's paying a last month's rent but we only heard on the last day of June and need to give two months' notice on our sardine-tin flat. And so, we move next week AGAIN. We still have no car purchased. We had been in the tiny flat precisely one week before we heard. If only our tenant

"Your career, in the holistic sense, is filled with transitions and change. The reality is that transitions will keep coming... keep identifying them and taking small steps towards living your mission."

Colleen Reichrath-Smith

had told us, we could have not bothered to spend all those weeks flat-hunting and could have moved directly back in. But hey, it's done. We are moving home. However, living here by the canal, a stone's throw from Chinatown – where the synagogue is now a mosque – feels so darn comfortable. So real. So normal. In a way we don't want to go back to the 'posh' part of town. Living in Malaysia changed us and being able to nip out for cheap halal lamb and lemongrass is what I have come to relish. Still, the chance of having my own bathroom with a window in it and a wardrobe big enough for my clothes is enticing. A terrace! A big cooker. A large fridge! Oh joy!

It can be so hard, can't it, watching our ATCKs get going on their careers? As a parent, I feel I know our son well and know what's best for him and as someone who can't keep things to myself, I tend to share. I realised this is often not helpful. When he was at school, Sam was good at most things – apart from sport and languages. He variously won the art prize, the geography prize and received top scores for his A Level Music Technology. He played guitar and actually stuck at the same instrument, unlike his brother, who switched instruments as often as we changed our bedsheets. Sam was in a band. He performed at the school fundraising concerts and loved music so much he used to blag free tickets from a local Hague website in exchange for writing about the gigs for them later. He got published in a few magazines including *The Weekly Telegraph* and *Transitions Abroad*. It was easy to assume he was a creative at heart, but his school Geography teachers had always told us, and him, that he was a born geographer.

He was told he should apply to Oxbridge, but he didn't want to and applied to the London School of Economics instead and got a place to study Social Geography. But specialising in one subject only was not what he wanted and so he left after the first year to study Liberal Arts in Utrecht. After that he did a Master's in Anthropology at University College London. So, you can see, he is an all-rounder who had been told he could do great things. Today, I believe that being told you can do great things is not helpful. He's one of those chaps who hates being told what to do – just like his father! Ian so hates being told what to do, because his parents used to tell him what to do, that he is incapable of doing something as simple as coming to the table because dinner is ready without doing something for himself first.

I'm learning painfully slowly that, as Khalil Gibran writes in *The Prophet*, "Your children are the arrows from which you as bows are sent forth. You cannot expect them to be like you, you can only strive to be like them."

Sam is leading his life his way and it is very hard for me to let go of the marionette strings and watch him work in a bar and a kitchen when he is capable of so much more. However, I realise that he is an ATCK, grew up in foreign countries where he was not fluent in the local language and never had a Saturday job as a teenager, like we all did. Maybe this is one reason why our ATCKs seem to take so long to get going in their lives compared to us. Different times, I know. Different times. And so, to shut myself up I like to list the great things he is achieving – he is busy, has a job, is earning money, has a social life, is brilliant at making friends, sings and plays the guitar beautifully with a voice like Leonard Cohen, rarely drinks, eats very nutritious food, can cook, runs (we are so lucky to be able to run to the beach here), does yoga, journals and does voluntary work. He is helping a couple of creatives with their grant applications. When I was his age I just had a job and a social life – oh, and a fiancé (Ian)! He has such a knack for detail while also being a creative soul, so I think this is a great direction for him. I know, though, that the moment I voice that thought it will probably shoot the idea dead in his mind. I'm learning, slowly, that it is not always helpful to give my kids ideas because they need to come up with ideas of their own. I'm such a control-freak though. I can't help myself trying to sow seeds in their minds. I'm such a networker that I can't help offering ideas and connections. Doing so seems to make Sam angry while Joshua appreciates it – for now at least!

I am so delighted to give Joshua some editing work and to be his writing mentor as he tries to make it as a freelancer. When I was his age I worked with my father. We had a partnership, writing computer manuals and teaching computers. We were both authors and both teachers. It was a magical time. We were never short of something to discuss and had so much in common that I know my poor mother felt cut out. My father was my mentor. My role model. He has written 31 books and it was always my goal to beat that. This book will be my 32nd. Now I know how marvellous it feels to be useful to your child and to watch them follow the same career path as you. I feel immensely privileged, but it is also a little weird because this is what I thought Sam would do. He was the one writing from an early age, not Joshua. Funny how things pan out.

By the time I write again, I will have moved house and be about to go off to England yet again, this time to take my mother to visit her brother, introduce Sam to baby Arthur and to go to Ian's aunt's summer family party. Family is so important. Friends are so important. I am so very thankful that we have both. It takes time, effort and often money to stay close to these people but boy does it make life better.

Canada? Going home at last? If you are like me, you'll find a way to make it work, in fact, you'll find a way to make it better than you ever dreamed.

Love until the next time,

Jo

Monday, July 17, Bangalore, India

Dear Jo,

Oh how your joy shone through! What a pleasure to hear about the happiness of sharing your city with a loved one, be it friend or family. I could picture your perfect days and was envious of the mission to gather your favourite foods. I have fond memories of cycling in our village when we lived near Gouda. To the various shops; to the butcher, the cheese shop, the greengrocer and oh, how heavenly was a visit to the baker!

I find it ironic that you write of food as we have concerns about ours at the moment; unfortunately, it isn't in the positive light that you're experiencing. Living in India is a compromise on many levels. You know my fear of the dangerous roads, which is somewhat of a manageable situation – limit travel by road and use the metro or train when possible. But the issues which are not easy to manage are the pollution and the food and water quality.

Not long after we moved to Bangalore, I started having allergy symptoms from the poor air quality. It manifests itself in eye and sinus irritations, often quite severe. I take a natural antioxidant, mangosteen, which helps to the point that I panic if I don't have a supply of it. After being back a week or two it sorts itself out, yet when I return from being away, I'm back to square one. I can't tell you how tedious and frustrating it is! Many of the large cities in India now compete with places like Beijing for the worst air quality possible – most people don't realise the high levels of toxins here in Bangalore.

Being genuinely concerned about the health implications, Bruce and I contend it's a blessing we're not here 12 months of the year. About six months after arriving, he began to monitor the air quality, which then prompted the purchase of an expensive air filter, then proper breathing masks to use for car or tuk-tuk travel. What is interesting is that despite the data reported occasionally in the newspapers, most everyone is either oblivious to the situation or chooses to ignore it. We've heard people comment that it's only a 'bit of dust'. In fact the fine pollutants, PM 2.5s, can work themselves into the bloodstream, the brain, and have irreversible implications. And so what most people don't know is that despite my beautiful canopy of trees that our living room and terrace look out to, for the most part the windows remain firmly closed… cocooned in the proverbial

"Most of us have space outside with natural light to have some potted herbs, tomatoes and now we even have vertical gardens. The most important point being, we need to make time to invest in our health."

Amanda Graham

'gilded cage.' Yesterday we threw caution to the wind and sat outside with morning coffee and a game of Scrabble; it was Sunday when the air quality is slightly better. The lush greenery and parakeets flitting through the canopy of trees belie the real story.

This is a painful admission, the fact that we're living in a country that could be compromising our health. It is difficult to admit to yourself and your family. Then yesterday we discovered reports concerning the quality of the food and water. Our water is filtered but with a constant water shortage in the fields, the story is that farmers use domestic effluent and industrial wastewater on vegetables. I've written about our vegetable *wallah* Raj. I have no idea where his vegetables come from and though they seem in good, fresh condition, the reports from NGOs raise the question... *what are we truly eating*? We manage it the best we can and have found some organic growers, but we're also thankful when we're away. It's a black cloud that hangs over our time here.

Part of us is relieved we won't be in Bangalore for four years after all, the initial period of this posting. I wrote of Canada next and yet you know as well as I do, Jo, the right job within the company may not materialise in the country you hope it might. And now just shortly after writing what we'd like to happen, especially Bruce, there could be a move mid next year to what would be one last location before home. We've declined to take another posting in Asia. There comes a time in an expat life when you don't want to compromise on issues like safety or pollution and I too am reminded of Maslow's *Hierarchy of Needs*. I know how often I become anxious in India; those health and safety needs feel constantly compromised. And so indeed, Jo, continue to embrace your surroundings as you are. Enjoy every bike ride, every scene on those cobblestoned streets that I also love.

We did 'escape' the city on the weekend and hiked to a 17th century fort. There were 13 of us as some of Bruce's team came along. These young and engaging Indian engineers are the future of this country and I truly loved being in their company. We spoke of ostentatious Indian weddings, the options to volunteer, I implored them to be a part of the solution to the trash and pollution problem, and I revelled in a good historical discourse. From the ramparts of the fort after a fairly arduous two-hour climb, we gazed down to the beautiful patchwork of farm fields dotted with ancient boulders and stalwart palm trees. We soaked in the view, chatted like old friends and breathed in the unpolluted air. It was all truly a breath of fresh air, figuratively and quite literally.

The mention of your small interim canal apartment and your home unexpectedly coming free (great news!), has taken me down memory lane. It's reminded me of our first 'home' in Japan. Bruce and I had backpacked through Asia and with only just enough money left for one more flight, we bought tickets from Hong Kong to Tokyo. We had just escaped from Tiananmen Square in Beijing and after six months on the 'road' we were ready to hang up our backpacks. We made our way to Osaka and a day later found jobs teaching English with Berlitz. After six months of travelling, overnight, threadbare cottons and worn sandals gave way to smart business attire. Quite surreal!

We lived in a hostel for a month, saving enough money

to move into a 'mansion'. It was really just a shoebox-sized apartment, but it was bliss. We could sleep in the same bed every night, shower every day, unpack our meagre belongings. And I remember them well: a few foot-high terracotta soldiers from Xian, soft camel-leather shoes from our safari through the Rajasthan desert and an elephant, an old wooden puppet from Thailand. And of course, a book collection. Even then I couldn't bear to not know the history of a place; clothes were given away to make more room in our backpacks for yet more books.

I remember the joy of that minuscule apartment with those few possessions arranged on a cardboard box. Our first piece of 'furniture' was a red futon. Sprinkled with a bamboo and lotus print, it brightened up the room, at least when it wasn't tucked away in its bespoke cupboard as is required in Japan. We lived in the modernity of the 'mansion' for about six months and then moved to an old Japanese apartment. It had *tatami* mats on the floors, *shoji* doors, and rats that visited between our apartment and upstairs… usually just when you sat down to dine with guests! Years later at a dinner with businessmen from Osaka, we told them where that second apartment had been. They were horrified. It was in the slums and dangerous, where the *yakuza* or gangsters lived. What had we been thinking? It was cheap, we told them. It was a little thrilling and it felt real, authentic.

Oh yes, I fully understand the sentiment of not wanting to leave the apartment that isn't in the 'posh' side of town. Yet you now have another neighbourhood you're familiar with, even though you'll soon be settled back into your own *buurt*. I agree there is something edifying about living in authentic surroundings. After all, is it not one of the reasons we live overseas; to experience other cultures and to be absorbed at least to some extent into that other world? This is one of the reasons we chose not to live in a compound in Bangalore, but on a street in the heart of the city. I admit that some neighbours have reminded me it is the most prestigious address in the city, 01, and the gleaming UB City mall and hotels attest to this. But certainly the odd rat, scattered trash and broken sidewalks easily contradict it. Nonetheless, I feel like I somewhat have a foot in both worlds. I love that vendors either call their 'cry', or set up on the side of the streets to sell their wares: fruits and vegetables, roasted groundnuts, sugarcane juice, or services of knife-sharpening, paper recycling and even brass polishing.

When I recall the decisions of where to live in previous countries, vignettes of memories unfold. Besides ensuring the children were settled in school, was there anything more crucial than finding the right place to live? Surely there wasn't! Case in point: when we moved to Qatar, our first true expat location. We had married in Canada while still living in Japan. A year later we bought our first house in The Netherlands, then one in Scotland, each was for a two-year period and on 'local terms'. Missing family, and Canada, we decided to move home – it lasted all of six months! An exciting overseas posting came our way and our wanderlust beckoned. Our family was incredulous. "We thought you were home for good," they despaired as they helped us pack up a lovely condo we had rented, the finishing touches on the decorating only just completed. But the pull was too strong and with two small children and one on the way, we accepted a job in Doha. It was our first true expat assignment – we thought we had died and gone to heaven!

Doha felt like a small town when we arrived in 1994. There were some gorgeous new compounds that a few friends lived in, but our housing allowance was more modest. We initially chose an independent home, yet it wasn't in a compound and it was lonely and isolated. A number of our friends lived in an older, livelier compound, and when I heard that a villa was soon to become available, I made it my mission to switch locations. Despite already having had our one and only move, I was determined. NBK Compound was the 'place to be'. Many families had children the same age as ours; the spacious bungalows were one storey with a gorgeous wrap-around terrace that felt like *Out of Africa*. They looked out to lush, scented gardens. Even without the supposed prerequisite pool and clubhouse, the compound had a certain charm and vitality to it.

"Bruce, we absolutely have to live in NBK, there's a villa coming free," I pleaded in desperation. "We made a mistake when we chose this house."

"It's impossible, Ter. You know we only get one move per location," Bruce reminded me.

"Yes, but a place wasn't available there when we arrived and soon there will be. Think of all the people we know living there. I feel completely left out where we are. What were we thinking?!"

"I agree, but that's the policy. I don't know what you want me to do."

I was desperate and concocted a plan, even if it meant telling a wee fib. I simply couldn't imagine not living in the 'right place' for four long years. We can convince ourselves of almost anything if we try hard enough and I believed that not living in NBK would impact our family's entire well-being.

"Bruce, how about this. I want you to plead my case and that it's actually in your best interest. You have to convince the housing people that you're worried about my mental health if I don't move into NBK. Tell them we have friends there and I'm 'fragile'. I need to be around more people. Tell them I can't cope with the kids on my own and need neighbours. Tell them anything but please, you have to get us into that compound."

To this day, I can't believe I was that desperate to live in that one specific place. And, of course, that I put Bruce under so much pressure.

It worked! Two months later we moved into what was truly a dream home. Oh, it was glorious with its frangipanis, prolific bougainvillea and marbled floors flowing out to the terrace. I decorated and painted. Bruce built the boys a pirate ship where there were seemingly no fewer than 10 or so 'pirates' scrambling up its gangplank at any one time. With the other families, we raised our children, we played, we partied, we camped... we became family. Four years of some of the happiest times of our life. It is absolutely true that the friends you make away from home can be as close, if not closer, than your own family. They see your children grow up on an intimate basis and live your everyday life with you. They are the ones you have the same references with; those wonderful seemingly far-fetched stories and the sometimes chaotic tribulations of that life. Anyone who lived there at that time surely knows the reference to a 'bad Doha day!'

When we moved out of that NBK home, Bruce and I stood arm in arm in the middle of the large empty living room. We were saying goodbye to more than a house; it was the backdrop of a beautiful family adventure. It was as if we could still hear the squeals and the laughter of the children as they ran round and round, through the house, through the walled garden. It echoed with the love that had swirled around its whitewashed walls. It was and will possibly be one of the best houses we've lived in. It wasn't our own, but it seemed to embrace us in every way. I am a firm believer of the importance that our surroundings play in our life. In Doha we had it all and, come to think of it, we've been pretty fortunate… there have been many 'almost perfect' homes scattered across the globe.

Remember I mentioned those 'heaps of Persian carpets'? I recall my mom and dad visiting us in that beloved home and Mom questioning a decorative purchase I was about to make. Not in a judgmental way, but it maybe seemed extravagant at the time. My mom recalls I was quite firm. "Whether we're here for six months or four years, Mom, it's our home. The boys need to feel that it isn't transient." For me, living in nine different countries has meant we needed some constants. We still pad across those same carpets and *kilims* purchased while in Doha and then Muscat. In fact, our kids have dibs on them – they remind them of home.

On that note, Jo, enjoy getting settled back into your home and safe trip back to England and your family. I'll enjoy the next few weeks before it's time to fly again. This trip will be

"As expats, we are the rare breed of people in small numbers that pack up and move from our nucleus and extended family members. So, yes, friends become family and go through all our ups and downs, illness of children, selecting schools, family picnics, holidays, weekend and going out, partying and more. It is the day to day that we share with friends."

Lesley Lewis

for a month and a half; time to check on that dear home of ours.

Much love,

Terry Anne

Mondays, July 24 and 31, Groenewegje, The Hague, The Netherlands

Dear Terry Anne,

Life, yet again, has got in the way of my bi-weekly email to you. I simply have not had any time to myself. More of that later, but first I need to tell you that I keep thinking about your comments in your previous email about you being of resilient stock. I'm still ruminating. I wonder how much your DNA and your family's history have affected your ability to handle the constant upheaval of being an expat family? My parents' families are from the UK for as far back as we can research. Ian's were British too, though his mother's family apparently came over from France yonks back. My father was born in London to London-born-and-bred folk. They only really moved round the East End and Essex. My mother still lives less than 15 miles from where she was born. I remember reading a book called *Work With*

Passion many years ago. It was by Nancy Anderson, and in it she suggested that we investigate the lives, beliefs and values as far back as our grandparents in order to gain an understanding of what might matter to us and help us work out our passions.

There is no doubt in my mind that the experiences of your mother's family have helped you all to be more resilient. Add to this mix that you and Bruce, while both being from Commonwealth countries, are from different continents. The Dutch blood that runs in your veins is likely to have caused you to be resourceful, efficient, pragmatic, practical and to appreciate beauty. Fascinating to think of it, really, isn't it? But now I wonder how much your 'history' has affected the way you have brought up your kids, who seem to be so much more resilient than ours, though all our kids' ability to switch languages and cultures and to slide between countries and cultures is certainly much better than ours as parents.

There is much talk of resilience being an acquired skill and, to a certain extent, I think that is right. But when I read what you wrote I wonder how much impact nurture and genetics have on our ability to be resilient. There is no doubt that we expats tend to mollycoddle our children. They rarely need to attend 'normal' schools with a cross-section of society, rarely encounter the issues associated with poverty. They have it easy. Often with housekeepers and nannies too. Taxis, drivers, folk who fold their clothes for them and do their washing. While many (my two particularly) have railed against the privileged lifestyle they have experienced, thanks to a father who perhaps appears to put work and money before family and does so by working for the devil (anything anti-eco, anti-sustainable, anti-socialist is not good in their eyes), they are still slow to do the washing up without being asked. It's interesting to ponder for sure. There's Joshua with his *pandan* wallet, wooden watch, recycled-lorry-tyre-cover washbag and fountain pen filled with 'green' ink, and Sam with his second-hand clothes and burning desire not to work in a traditional role. What have we done?! I write that with a wry smile. As Philip Larkin wrote in his poem, 'They fuck you up, your mum and dad'. I concur.

When we began our emails back in May, I thought we were going to focus on the adult kids' part of the expat empty nest, but what has transpired is that our boys are just a part of what is very much a whole. A whole host of issues surrounding being an expat in our fifties. Sure, we talk about our kids and our ageing parents – they were the topics I thought would be in the forefront – but we are also discussing our retirement, the uncertain futures our husbands face and our own burning desires to be fulfilled professionally. Our age and the health issues that come with that, our knowledge that we need to look after our bodies, minds and souls and our deep love of travel. I expect these are common themes for many others of our age, don't you? Fascinating, isn't it?

Since I last wrote, our shipment has arrived in our house. Ian (who is pretty stressed from all these moves and trips to the UK as well as an incredibly busy role at work) could not find his bike key that morning and so I was there alone to receive the truck. When he did eventually arrive, he stayed for one hour and had to go back to work for a meeting. When he returned he brought his laptop and stood in the kitchen piled high with boxes, balancing his keyboard on a

"With all the pressures
of family life, let
alone the challenge
of transition issues,
making sure as Steven
Covey says, you try to
'understand first and
then be understood'."

Ian Moody

box at nose height. I wonder why he bothered coming at all! Joshua and I worked for 10 hours that day. Sam joined for a few hours too. The next day Ian went to England to buy a car and visit his parents. Joshua and I did another full day with the shippers who were now unpacking. Then we spent the whole weekend there. After four days the house was still indescribable, piles of boxes and paper everywhere and still a hundred boxes left to go. We were exhausted but boy oh boy, do I love that house! The high ceilings, the light, the chats over the balcony to our wonderful neighbours, the familiar shops, the William Carlos Williams poem on the wall of the hotel opposite. Yet, as our tenant has paid July's rent, we are not officially able to move in until tomorrow. Of course, we have no Internet and heaps of boxes but we will be in! The gorgeous Chinese furniture we bought in KL does not fit in the rooms. We cannot find homes for things so have a room, the smallest bedroom, that our shippers christened The Ebay Room and crammed it with stuff we are going to have to offload. The sofa we had on the balcony in KL has to go in our dining room, which means we have no room for the table – seriously!

Moving and unpacking happened, as I said, seeing neither hide nor hair of Ian. I was baking hot and hot-flushy, blaring out BBC Radio 4 podcasts or the radio (thank God for 3G), but happy.

But back to England, remember? We unloaded the shipment, returned to the tiny flat and Ian went away. As I write this Ian has WhatsApped that we now own a car and he is doing the ironing for his father. He is not happy. The car he had driven a few hundred miles from Yorkshire to his parents in Surrey had turned out to be a dud in need of new tires and a differential. He'd spent most of his previous weekends researching cars online and so this was a massive blow – mostly to his ego I expect. As a result, he had to take some days off work in order to visit a local garage and the Citizens Advice Bureau and take a couple of days' holiday in order to return the car all the way to Yorkshire and get his money back. Meanwhile the boys and I were heading to England in yet another hire car to take my mother to see her brother in Broadstairs on the Kent coast for two nights. It's become an annual tradition that we take her to visit her wonderful, God-loving, eccentric, messy, metaphorical, musical, deliciously mad brother, Rob. The boys adore Uncle Rob but my ex-maths teacher, serial thinking, binary father fails to understand a word he says. The only way we can get my mother to allow herself to visit the brother she adores is to accompany her, while she leaves my confused 89-year-old father at home with Betsy the miniature dachshund.

We break through the drooping hollyhocks and weeds to get to Rob's front door and have a magical time of fish and chips and improvisation at his dusty grand piano. Always a trip to quirky Margate to visit the Turner Contemporary Gallery and a visit to my cousin Alison, who at 48 has just produced Rob's only grandchild, George. She makes the most amazing cakes and despite having a 12-week-old baby had made us a glorious polenta and raspberry Victoria sandwich and a sticky ginger beetroot cake.

Sam, Joshua, Granny and I all shared a family room at the Botany Bay Hotel, right by the cliffs, woken at dawn by the cry of gulls and the tang of seaweed and the hush of the sea slipping in through the windows. We wandered on the beach at low tide and found the coast's mysterious

"Never forget that for many TCKs, the sense of home is most often defined in terms of relationships, not place per se."

Ruth Van Reken

holey chalk pebbles had become entangled with emerald or magenta weeds and now resembled the heads of wraiths. My mother was in her element, beachcombing and creating daft scenes out of our sea creatures. We made a reindeer, a punk band and a goddess. Uncle Rob lay down and soon had seaweed hair coming out of his ears and a seaweed halo. Pure magic. Being creative, behaving like children, on the seashore was the perfect antidote to our constant moves and repeated drives through the Channel Tunnel.

Being together, three generations of the family, is precious. Whenever you write of your family times I can sense the joy and connectedness you feel. We are very lucky to be able to do this and regularly. And so we enjoyed two nights and three days of heaven while Ian cared for his parents and had an abortive, expensive car-buying trip that left him five holiday days poorer. We fetched Ian from the train station near my parents on his return from Yorkshire – luckily with his money back for the car. Our next job: to go to the storage facility we had used to store the contents of the boys' London flat, our winter clothes and extra-thick bedding before we headed out to Malaysia four years ago.

"You are our favourite kind of client," joked Carl, the MD of Steele's storage, the next day. "You pay us eight pound a week to look after crap you don't really need and don't have time to sort through!"

Yup, that was us. Ian had arrived by then and it took six hours and two cups of tea to plough through stuff we'd not missed for four years. Carl gave me my strong builder's tea in a plain white mug with the words *I Am a Twat* on the base that appeared to onlookers each time I took a sip. I know English humour can baffle many foreigners. The way we delight in being very rude, almost cruel to others, is to us, the sign that we are accepted. I am not surprised others fail to understand this, but it gave Ian and I sense of belonging, a sense of home, a sense of being normal. We needed the laugh as we removed everything from two separate containers and chose which pile was for Holland, which was the kind of 'crap' Carl mentioned and which would go straight into his skip. We found bags of clothes infested with flying insects, pillows yellow with mould, shoes and handbags bent into such odd shapes we'd never use them again. The company will allow us one delivery to Holland from home base and we were jolly well going to use it! The boys stayed at Granny and Grandpa's and did not come with us to Steele's. Were they lazy or wise? I sent them photos of items so they could tell us whether to chuck, save or send. I expect the upshot of this will be that in another month or two we'll be paying Carl another 75 quid to open the container again so they can fish out items they wished we'd fetched this time.

We had half an hour free before it was time to turn around and head for London, to visit our new surrogate grandbaby, Arthur. Becky, his mum, if you remember, has become such a good friend that she calls me Mum II. After three hours in traffic I scooted straight into the sitting room and scooped him up. There is nothing like having a baby in your arms for all to be right with the world. We played 'pass the baby' for a couple of hours and then headed off to stay with friends. And on and on and on.

Life 'back home' for the expat is just a round of racing from one set of important people to another, quick heartfelt hugs, repeated conversations and off to the next lot. Squeezing in some important things along the way counters the drudgery bits and I was delighted to meet up with Anne who I wrote about last month and has bought a flat in Hammersmith. We walked in Hyde Park and visited the Grayson Perry exhibition at The Serpentine Gallery. As you said, Terry Anne, over that snatched breakfast at the KL Le Meridien when you were passing through a year or so back, "our expat life has crushing lows and fabulous highs and the lows are the price we pay for the highs."

Meanwhile, as the R word returns and returns to our minds we are constantly wondering what to buy, whether to buy, where to live and how to make money when we retire. Ian doubts he'll have a job up to retirement age and we have to think carefully and long term. The trouble is, having travelled so much and seen so much we find it easy to imagine ourselves 'at home' in so many places, and this makes the decision impossible. In the last year, we have nearly bought a flat in London, seriously considered a house in Stamford and almost bought a flat in Penang. In the last week, I have imagined myself in Margate, Broadstairs, Devon, France and Stamford and looked at properties on Right Move in all of them. In the last 24 hours, we've considered selling our house in Holland and using the money for something in the UK and also not selling it but renting it out permanently and living off the profit. Ian has a copy of *Retire to the Life You Love* on his bedside table, and last night in our bijou canal apartment Joshua lay in his weeny room under the eaves shouting ideas down to us in the sitting room.

"Why don't you run a bed and breakfast? I could see you doing that."

"You could have fun growing veg and cooking it, Mum, if you had a garden."

"Yeah, I could see you running a glamping site."

"I know! An eco B & B!"

This December will mark our 30th wedding anniversary and our 30th year on the move. It's been a time of great highs and great lows. And now we cannot make our bloody minds up what to do at the end of this short two-year posting.

So, you see, I really have been way too busy to write earlier. In fact, when I think about it… if I have time to think about it… I realise that I have not yet had a normal week this year. It's August tomorrow and so far I have been saying goodbye, packing up, living in two hotels, two transit apartments, moving in, driving the 10-12 hours back to my parents in England five times, travelling to Penang, Langkawi, Dubai and France and living out of a suitcase.

I shall say this here… THIS IS THE LAST TIME. I AM NOT DOING IT AGAIN! IT TAKES UP TOO MUCH LIVING TIME.

Still, mostly it has been fun!

I hope all is well with you as you plan your summer trip to Canada, Terry Anne, and the roundabout goes round and round and round.

Love,

Jo

Monday, August 14, Whistler, British Columbia, Canada

Dear Jo,

Like you a few weeks ago, it's been difficult to find time to write during our vacation. Thank you for those lovely and familiar images – the work of unpacking and the joy of seeing a home come together, that of rooting through years of stuff that supposedly needed rescuing in storage and the beautiful imagery of precious time with family. And I chuckle at your mention of picturing yourself living in various places and which do you choose! I write this from Whistler, British Columbia. People from around the world stroll past my perch on a flower-infused outdoor patio. They wander leisurely as the locals wheel mountain bikes and walk dogs around their happy but hindering masses. This is a world-renowned ski town, an hour or so drive from Vancouver. But the summer is all about mountain biking, rock climbing, canoeing and long summer nights of relaxing with a cold beer or glass of wine.

We made our way here after a few days in Vancouver with Luke and Trixie. We also wined and dined with her parents; we get along fabulously! The 'kids' then joined us for a few days here, where we canoed on crystal clear lakes, cycled along mountain trails, whilst having to divert hefty black bears. We visited art galleries and dined on superb Pacific Coast salmon. Yes, I could live here in a heartbeat. But wonderfully, we can visit often; it's a gorgeous ten-hour meander from Kimberley. And yes, you can well imagine the contrast from India!

I had arrived home a week before Bruce and after a wonderful visit with my parents, made my way to our house. Not wanting me to drive on my own to Vancouver, Luke flew to Kimberley to join me. We tidied up the garden, caught up with neighbours and after a few days of *home sweet home*, had a leisurely drive to Vancouver. Happily detouring through Canada's wine region along the way, this oldest child of mine never fails to enlighten, to entertain, to listen, to fill me with love.

"We're camping on the way, Mom," Luke had announced, throwing a tent and a few sleeping bags in the back of the SUV. We drove through mountain passes, dramatic and glorious. We encountered a moose clopping across the highway, leading her calf to a refreshing emerald green lake. We tasted excellent reds and whites in Oliver, Canada's wine capital – one could be in Tuscany or Napa Valley. It was heavenly, as was the tangerine-orange sun that rose over the campsite and seemed to pierce the tent with its luminosity.

How wonderful, a road trip with my 26-year-old. Time alone, to catch up, to laugh, to do what we've always done as mother and son; we're very close. Luke is my joyful 'child'. Is it because he's the eldest? Is it genetic? Is it because he was in one place for six years through junior and senior high, unlike his brothers?

"Before blame is assigned, remember each child has lived a unique life. Families moved at different times in each child's development process... as parents we cannot compare our children but must seek to understand each one's personality and story."

Ruth Van Reken

Of our three sons, Luke is the one who has navigated life with seeming ease and success. A four-year degree in International Relations, a Master's Degree from Sweden in Sustainability Science. An internship in Calgary, then Singapore. All a tremendous amount of effort and yet not one misstep. He now finds himself in Vancouver, because of love, delaying a 'real job'. Instead, he's on-set as an extra in Vancouver's busy film industry. Last week found him on three different sets: on the beach at a toga party for a TV show, one of the gang members on the hit series *Riverdale* (a take on the old Archie comics) and as a 'beautiful person' at a red carpet event in the filming of *The Arrangement*, about Tom Cruise's marriage. On and on it goes, it is never dull hearing of his latest exploits. He and his girlfriend Trixie, an assistant to a film producer, often escape city life to climb and camp in the majestic environs of Vancouver. They plan to move to Europe in the new year, let's hope that first career job is on the horizon!

But for now, it's hard to describe the joy I feel for Luke and I realise that he is doing what Bruce and I did at about the same age: living spontaneously and gathering more life experiences. Needless to say we're supportive, contending that it's a long life to focus on a career.

On that long road trip I asked Luke why he hadn't struggled like his brothers.

"I don't know, Mom, it was never an option not to succeed."

We talked about six years in one country, through junior and high school.

"To be honest I always felt a little cheated that I hadn't been at an International School through high school, like Andrew. He got to travel, play sports throughout Europe. I was in Katy, Texas."

This is the first I've heard of this and then I recall that it had almost been a different scenario. With Luke going into his Senior year of high school in mind, we had declined a move. I recall the stressful details as if it was yesterday. After much deliberation, Bruce had accepted a job in Kuala Lumpur that summer and we had listed the house for sale. We must have spoken to the boys about the decision and I'm sure there was acceptance. Bruce went off for initial meetings and to house search. We'd be there in a few months just in time to start school – spots had been secured for each of the boys.

Not long after arriving in KL Bruce calls home.

"Ter, we have to talk, this isn't going to work."

"What do you mean? You've already accepted the job. There's an offer on the house, I need to sign the papers in three days."

"I know, but now being here, I don't see how I can take the boys out of that environment, to this. Luke drives two minutes to school, he'll be back on a bus for an hour each way here. He's the captain of the hockey team, Matt's on that team. They both play ball and they're on the golf team. What the hell were we thinking, taking them away from all of that? And Andrew, look at his budding baseball career."

We went back and forth, round and round for three days over expensive phone calls. The pros, the cons, the implications.

I was distraught. Suddenly we had not one, but three offers on the house. If we were staying, I had schools to cancel in KL, ones to re-instate in Katy. The packers and movers had been booked, we had started saying our farewells. As expats we try to time our moves around our children's schooling. We know how it goes: don't move your kids in their last two years of high school. We were about to do just that. The other two weren't at a 'critical' juncture.

On the last day possible, it was Bruce who made the decision. "I can take one for the team, but I won't do this to the kids. The move is off. I've told the company we need one more year in Houston."

I remember gathering the boys around me and breaking the news to them. They were silent for a moment, stunned... yes, talk about having to build resilience of character without any choice! I think the first one to say something was Matt: "Okay great, can I play on that travel hockey team, then?" And with that, we all got back on with our lives. Matt was nominated Captain of that hockey team which boosted his confidence and helped his improving attitude. Luke had a brilliant last year of high school. It strikes me now how easily we all adjusted, just changed our mindset overnight. As you've mused, Jo, I do believe resilience is fostered as well as inherited. Most definitely.

So the news that some part of Luke wished we had gone to KL came as a surprise.

"I was always envious when I was in university and you guys were living in Norway. All the travelling. Andy always here and there. Mom, come on, his grad party was in Spain.

"To help you make the best decision for the family, do a PMI – Positives, Minuses, Interesting – which will help you work out what to do."

Ian Moody

Mine was in Galveston, with chaperones and a no alcohol policy. It's too embarrassing to even think about!"

It dawned on me that each of my kids had had a completely different high school experience. Luke in Texas, Matt at a boarding school in Canada the last two years, and Andrew in Norway. I'm curious as to how much this also shaped them. How many expat families struggle with the timing of school years as they try to accommodate all the children? How many kids are torn from all they love to a great unknown at such an important age? How many teenagers rue the fact that once they graduate, often their parents move, and bang, just like that you have no base to return to? Luke's hometown of six years disappeared overnight when he went to university in Canada and we moved to Norway. His friends, however, reunited back in Katy during the holidays. I remember how difficult it was for him, how he missed them. Eventually it got easier, month by month, by year.

And yet he admits these experiences have made him stronger and he accepts it for what it was, and is. Luke has an easy-going personality and again you wonder. How much of how we deal with things is simply genetics, despite being raised in the same family? To see Luke today with degrees in his back pocket, myriad experiences, with strong principles and as someone who is most definitely in the driver's seat of his life – well, as a parent you smile wide, very wide. You count your blessings and you give the tall kid a big hug as often as you can!

Love for now, Jo,

Terry Anne

Monday, August 21, Bankastraat, The Hague, The Netherlands

Dear Terry Anne,

Oh my goodness, how I remember those schooling conundrums and conversations. The should-we-shouldn't-we of moving and accepting (and declining) postings. As a family you seem to be so cohesive. I am impressed that Bruce was able to put the family first when so many husbands in his position can't bring themselves to do that. I expect it makes them think they will look weak. I think of your experience when you were determined to move in Doha and how Bruce stepped up to the plate then too. I remember once when the company called Ian on the first day of our long-awaited home leave, many years ago when we were in Oman, and told him they needed him back. He told them no way was he going back and he'd quit if he had to. They backed down. We make decisions that we think are right for the children.

Between our Norway and Netherlands postings we lived back in the UK for seven years, near where I grew up, and my parents. Ian commuted to work but he felt sidelined in our family life and though, ultimately, he managed a four-day week so he could spend more time with us, the arrangement did not make any of us happy. When our beloved next-door neighbour died of cancer, it broke our hearts and was the last straw. We could not live most of the week apart from each other any longer and so we all moved to the Netherlands. The boys were 12 and 13, at an age when their peers were becoming more important to them than their parents. They were doing well in school, with Joshua engaged in every sport possible. They had friends. And then we upped sticks to The Hague. It seemed such a good idea at the time – the right idea, and right for us as a family – but, actually, I'm not sure it was right for both the children. Sam found friends fast but Joshua floundered for a year until he had a friend who 'got' him. Later, he made a superb friend, a real buddy, but at 15 Joel's family moved to Singapore and Joshua was left bereft.

The same thing happened to me, at 13, and again at 16, when my best friends left not the same country as me, but my school. Doug Ota writes in his book, *Safe Passage*, about how difficult it is for the kids left behind, or the *movee* as he calls them. I blame the fact that I felt 'abandoned' by my best friends for my lack of self-esteem. I wonder if Joshua feels the same. When we left England he lost not one or two best mates, but whole swathes of them: his teammates. I know now that these experiences leave our children with unresolved grief. We parents say, they only lost a friend, they'll make new ones, what's the big deal? But it is a big deal.

Ah, those highs and lows we write of, likewise the positives and negatives. In leaving England we had a better standard of living, more holidays, more time as a family and a new language. But we lost firm friends, familiarity, grandparents round the corner and the wonderful countryside around us. Our choices have shaped us, made us strong and made us vulnerable and thrown up a host of *roads less travelled* to go down.

But our decisions are our decisions, we made them with the tools and knowledge we had at the time. A mother is only as happy as her unhappiest child and so, for a while, we regret some of those choices. Right now, I am delighted to be back in Holland as a family again, and, you know, the boys are too. This house was once our home and can be once again.

When you move into a Dutch house they have so many floors and such narrow stairs that the furniture comes in through the windows. Ian and I had spent ages deciding what would go where as we lay in bed one morning in our canal house. The trouble is that we had forgotten how many doors and windows we have and almost everything is now not only in the wrong room but on the wrong blasted floor!

We moved in on 2nd August and Ian was not impressed with how we'd directed those removal men – well then, he should have been there, right?! Of course, it was my fault!

I write this on 21st August. My mother's 82nd birthday. They have just been to stay with us for 10 days and it's been a privilege to have them. However, when they booked their flights we had not known we would have a rush move on our hands and that they would arrive about a week after we did. Not good timing! With Ian not at his best until his 'space' is organised, and both boys here too, Sam had to give up his hard-won bedroom to Granny and Grandpa and curl up on a sofa in a room surrounded by boxes. Like Ian, he needs his space in order to have peace of mind. Joshua has no mattress yet and is sleeping on a duvet on the floorboards,

"Everyone has a choice on how to behave. Reframe your cognitive beliefs and this in turn will change your behaviour... So ask yourself, and define joy."

Lesley Lewis

having made his own wardrobe out of two Indonesian ladders and a bundle of bamboo. His drawers are old fruit crates. My eco-warrior! My father is getting increasingly frail. He can walk without a stick but a kilometre is about his max. Thank God he can still manage our endless Dutch stairs. Away from home he loses confidence, forgets words and looks rather lost much of the time. My mother just worries about everything and everyone, takes on everyone else's stress (some of which she imagines, some not) and so she gets herself a nice bout of cystitis, which she refuses to bother us with and so gets increasingly tight-lipped. Yup, that's my family!

My pa used to have friends in Rotterdam and visit them with his old school chums, all of whom have now passed on. For years he has talked about his visits to the wealthy Tauw family and their post-dinner trips to De Pijp bar. This time we decided to find out if it still existed and take him there. We were completely stunned to discover it was not only still there but still had its walls festooned with ties and beermats.

"That's where we used to sit!" he exclaimed. "Pete Mellors and me and the Tauw family!" It was wonderful to see him reliving such happy times. Another evening was *Jazz an de Gracht* and we sat by the canal at a super café and were entertained by one band boat after another, all evening. This trip we increasingly see the benefits of living here. We love our house. We love our neighbourhood. We know the folk in the shops downstairs and they too feel like family. All of us shop in the health shop that inhabits the ground floor of our building wearing our slippers. This week they lent me a vacuum cleaner and a broom. That is what I call belonging. This feels like home.

And so, as I juggle having houseguests, feeding six every evening, keeping my parents entertained and my husband appeased, fitting in my own work has been tough. 'Twas ever thus. I usually allow myself two hours in the morning at my desk, but that only gives me the time to 'firefight' and answer emails.

We still have no car, but – Holland being so green and forward-looking – we signed up with a carshare scheme called Greenwheels. I paid a refundable deposit of €255 and then three of us can sign up and help ourselves to one of about 10 little red 'buzzboxes' in our neighbourhood. A 'buzzbox' is my family speak for a cheap and cheerful little car. One flash of my *OV-chipkaart* (travel pass) at a box on the windscreen and the door opens. I pay €4 an hour plus 27 cents a kilometre. It is a lifesaver!

The day after my folks left I lay on the sofa for hours watching telly. I was exhausted. Ian finally got round to sorting some boxes and I revelled in cooking for just two again as the boys had driven to Berlin for the weekend to collect Sam's stuff that he had left there in March.

Meanwhile, I read Kristin Louise Duncombe's *Trailing – a Memoir* on my iPad. I met her at FIGT earlier this year and picked up her *Five Flights Up* to read, not realising that it was the second of her memoirs. I was impressed. She writes such compelling stuff, useful too, for being a psychotherapist, mother and expat, she knows what kind of issues will resonate with the reader and ensures she remains authentic and vulnerable at all times. Anyway, I loved *Five Flights Up* about her time in Lyon and Paris and so asked Kristin if we could do a book swap. I'd read her *Trailing* if she read my *Sunshine Soup* (my own kind of memoir disguised as fiction). We struck up an online friendship and I must say, the Internet is great for networking, isn't it? You make firm friends so fast! *Trailing*, if anything was even more raw than *Five Flights*. A new wife and a TCK herself, life in Africa was not easy. She suffered anxiety, depression, panic attacks, doubts about her marriage, worked with AIDS sufferers and was car-jacked among many other things. But through it all, she was, is, a psychotherapist and that is what made her book so terrific for me. Towards the end, now with a baby girl, Kristin is asked to do a talk at an expat event. In the book she lists what she considers to be the main issues faced by expat wives:

Interesting, isn't it? I am SO darn impressed with that woman that I have just interviewed her for my websites about the issues that concern so many other writers with a story: how can I be vulnerable without looking stupid? Should I name my children? What stories deserve to be heard? I tell you, reading is so inspiring for me. I love reading expat memoirs – when they are good. Laura Stephens, with her *An Inconvenient Posting*, is similar for she too is a therapist. Then there are all the amazing Robin Pascoe books, of course. *Global Mom* by Melissa Dalton-Bradford. *Harvesting Stones* by Paula Lucas. The best memoirs, to my mind, inspire, support, inform and entertain as does all writing that I believe to have value. But, I guess that was a digression from the other stuff in my life.

Now we are 'home' in the country we have lived in as a family longer than anywhere else and in a house that we own and so we can bang in nails to our heart's content. Here I have friends who are permanent, married to locals, working here in normal jobs. They are not going to leave anytime soon. All stuff that 'normal' folk take for granted but now I am here, sitting at my desk in my office, in our house for which we pay the mortgage and all the bills; it feels good. Very good.

Joshua meanwhile is off to Indonesia for a month in an Islamic school fostering East-West relations while blogging about it, courtesy of a British Council/ Embassy initiative. He will leave straight from France and be gone a month.

When I read your last letter it makes it so apparent that to others our lives must seem so charmed and our issues 'luxury' issues. Only those of us who are 'in' this peripatetic life can appreciate exactly how high our 'highs' are (like those you wrote of) and just how low, how tough, how heartbreaking the 'lows' are. Maybe it happens with age, that now I can appreciate things I never noticed before: things like my own four walls, the amazing entertainment on offer in the Netherlands, being able to borrow things from neighbours, speaking (ish) the language, knowing how things work (ish) and being able to read the signs that tell me how much my fine will be if I fail to put my cardboard inside the correct recycling bin. Small pleasures too, get bigger, here in this third age of my life.

On Friday we all go on holiday to a small chateau in the Dordogne with two other families. We met them all over 20 years ago when we lived in Oman. Next week, thirteen of us, with children aged from 21 to 26 will be together. I count my blessings.

With love,

Jo

Monday, August 28, Kimberley, British Columbia, Canada

Dear Jo,

Like you in your happy and familiar home in The Hague, I am filled with joy as the summer draws to a close. I write from the deck of our home in beautiful British Columbia. I peer through tall pines out to the ski hill and watch deer munch on my parched grass. I gaze at the lines of our home's tall timbers, following them to their highest peak; they give the home its 'chalet' appearance. Just newly varnished, their knotted wood is rich and strong and stable. Perhaps they represent what this home means to us: warmth and stability. Perhaps this mountain town of Kimberley was meant to anchor our global lives and soothe our often-fragile souls.

Kimberley was once home to one of the largest lead-zinc mines in the world, even its name was changed in 1896 in the hopes that it would achieve success as its namesake in South Africa had done. Besides mining, it has something else that has attracted people from far and wide to its location sandwiched between two mountain ranges: a ski hill, fishing, hiking, acclaimed golf courses and nearby lakes for paddling. Eight years ago, it became our home base.

Living in Houston at the time, a ski trip brought us to Kimberley's family-friendly ski hill. A fateful stop to view the show home at a new development, close to its base, would seal our fate. Once a campground, *Dreamcatcher's* two narrow roads meander through pine and aspen trees that surround mountain-style homes, all with the nearby backdrop of the Rocky Mountains. We were immediately smitten. The decision was immediate… *wherever we are in the world, this is where we'll return.* When Bruce and I ventured back outside after the 'sales talk', all three boys were lying in the snow – their widening legs and flapping arms forming snow angels. Their laughter filled the cold December air as their gazes fixed on the stars above. We knew in that moment it was the right decision; this would be home.

And, like you, we are part of the community. We know the shopkeepers, the bartenders at the ski hill, the marshals at the golf courses, and the neighbours, amongst whom are many good friends. We are welcomed home every visit – drinks on the deck and barbecues, invitations to golf or snow-shoe depending upon the season. And there are the friendly hellos throughout the town, "Hey, you're back. How long this time? Aren't you ready to stay put?"

There is also the acknowledgement that, while we're here, family time is precious. And so this morning the house is eerily quiet. I'm on my own after treasured time with Bruce, Luke and Trixie, Andrew and Ayla, and my parents (Matt has remained in India.) Despite the silence, the laughter and love still drift through the rooms and warms my heart. If it wasn't dining on the deck with fine BC wine, it was playing games or chatting heart to heart. There was camping, kayaking, the guys trekking down the hills on mountain bikes, walking in the woods. The beauty of it all? Our grown children can't get here fast enough nowadays.

How often do expats struggle with where they'll retire or return home to while they're still abroad? At some point, you can no longer impose at Grandma and Grandpa's house with your teenage children. And you want to create your own family memories, in your own home. We truly got lucky. But I find that poses problems as well. Where once we all gathered at my mom and dad's acreage, our time there is now limited and they feel the absence keenly. They pine for the days when six grandchildren played from dawn to dusk and family gathered around their ample dining table. Now it's mostly just the two of them and our visits are never long enough. My parents are about 10 years younger than yours are, Jo, but I keenly hear your words and worries. The concern for our parents' well-being in later life is more acute when we don't live next-door or close by, in the same country, or even in the same continent as is our case.

I haven't told my parents yet that we won't be home for Christmas, that we've decided to take advantage of living in an exotic part of the world. The kids are coming to India and hopefully we'll hop over to Oman – our favourite place that we've lived. They can revisit one of their childhood homes, re-live trips to the desert and actually visit a school they attended. I know it's now accepted that this is a good thing for TCKs, to revisit a place they once called home. We're all excited about the visit.

Unfortunately, it becomes another 'break' with my parents, more time spent in the nucleus of our immediate family. My mom and dad often make the four-hour drive from their house here to Kimberley, but those trips are becoming less frequent as we become busier when we're home. If in fact we're there at all. There is a constant 'tug of war' for time. And now with two girlfriends in our family, things have changed even more.

As a mother of three sons, I admit it is wonderful to have other women in the house. As a tomboy growing up, I always wanted sons, but yes, the odd person has actually asked, "Didn't you want girls?" When we decided to have our third, it was to have another child, not necessarily a girl. But still, it's a joy to have female company in the house and diffuse all that masculinity (you'll know all about this too, Jo!). Bruce and I feel close to Ayla and Trixie and we've watched Luke and Andrew build futures with strong, talented young women who make them happy. They've embraced us with open arms, as we have them.

"I love you, Terry," Ayla said as she hugged me late one evening recently, "and I love you too for your storytelling." She listens to my 'adventures' and was thrilled when she happened to be with me while I was interviewing for a blogpost.

"Andrew," she later said, "I love being with your mom. There's always someone to talk to, always something going on." I write this not to boast or to embellish, only to emphasise that as a mother of sons, you are often told… *if your son's partner doesn't like you, you're in trouble!* I have never truly worried about this, yet I can assure you the palpable relief you feel when you truly like and respect their partners and it is reciprocated.

"You have to learn to 're-family' at every stage of life. When your kids go to college, when they marry, when the first grandchild comes, your family dynamics will change. Remember, you aren't losing the past, but look for ways to re-family for the present and the future."

Ruth Van Reken

As I write, Bruce is back in Vancouver helping the gang move apartments and he's thrilled to be doing it. Sure the holiday is over, but helping with everyday things like packing up and moving are milestones that you want to be a part of in your adult children's lives. And I see history repeating itself. Where not too long ago it was my parents helping us, it's now our turn to be there for our kids. I also know that in the not too distant future, we'll be assisting my mom and dad. Goodness knows they've helped us enough times!

So we have found a place to eventually retire to, but now my parents, or at least one of them, would like a new stage in that retirement. Despite enjoying the gardening their acreage requires, part of my mom wants to relocate before it becomes too burdensome. She wants to get out more. She yearns to be more sociable than my dad is. At 74, she wants one more chapter in life. Maybe a condo in the city, more travelling, more excitement?

"Of course, go ahead and travel," my dad told her when I visited recently. "I'm not stopping you at all, I'm happy for you to go." And he is perfectly fine with her travelling on her own, but that isn't necessarily the answer.

"I'm happy being here. I've got the best spot on earth, and my dogs," he said contentedly. He was referring to the acreage and the aged dog at his side – sadly our two spaniels had retired there but have since passed away. In fact, we were sitting on the exact spot where Bruce and I were married. It's a beautiful acreage filled with treasured memories, but my mom feels the walls closing in on her. She feels time knocking at the door. I asked what we could do. Maybe sell our condo in Calgary and put the money towards one in the city that she could jaunt off to?

"Your dad won't leave here until he doesn't have a choice," mom insisted. So despite a mostly good marriage, there are days when she envisions a different life. She often gets homesick all these years later, and misses her roots back in Holland. It's unlike her to be down and when I related what the kids were up to, the comings and goings, instead of being engaged, this particular evening, she shook her head. "I can't keep up with it all," she said resignedly. I gently reprimanded her but realised that life, especially ours, seems to be moving too fast.

"Mom, this isn't like you. I'm so sorry I'm not here for you more." The next morning, she was herself again and gave me a long hug, "I just needed to talk about it, honey, I'm fine." But of course, I worry, and Jo, it is so true. Sometimes we just need to share, to lighten the burden. It can be through talking, and as we know, it can be through writing.

I realise more and more the cycles of life are replaying themselves through the generations and despite being there for my parents as best I can, I walk the fine line of balancing the new norm in our family with my concern for them. This seems to be the most important aspect to hold on to, as you say, in the third stage in life… to count our blessings, yet to somehow make it all work, for everyone. With the new reality in our family of different locations to visit our children, of girlfriends (with the hope that Matt too will find someone to share his life with), I am thankful for every moment with my parents. Yet, I know deep down, it isn't enough. It will never be enough.

This will be an ongoing 'struggle' as you've also written about, Jo, indeed we have written of so much. It has not always been joyful, but it is fascinating how effortlessly the

"As a global nomad,
I think guilt is a very
strong emotion that tugs
at the heart strings all
the time."

Ian Moody

words and stories have flowed. How organically we have meandered from one topic to another. How therapeutic it has been to write and share: the joys, the issues and heartbreaks, the reflections of our global life, and all that tough stuff!

As I gaze out to robins darting amongst my pines and to sunflowers nodding in the afternoon sun, I'll finish with the sentiments of Luke and Trixie. It was Trixie's first visit here and their words encapsulate all that is important; really, all that we can hope to create in life. Not only did they leave a thank-you card, they each penned a message in my guestbook. The same book even I write in each time I'm home – I've done this since the day we claimed it as our home base. Yes, just to capture life's moments in writing for posterity. Jo, we both know the beauty and power of that!

Dear Terry Anne and Bruce,

This weekend has been such a lovely introduction to Kimberley. I now know why this place is so special to Luke and the Wilsons. Thank you for the welcome dance as I strolled through the front door and the glass of wine within two minutes! I enjoyed the family stroll through the town Platzl, flipping through the photo albums, seeing the family cross-stitch collection and learning the story or meaning behind every piece of furniture. Finally finding myself at the scene of the family anecdotes you've shared was the perfect way to spend the year mark of meeting Luke. Thanks for raising Luke to be so thoughtful and family-orientated, amongst so many other things. I hope we have much more adventuring and more late night conversations ahead. Thank you for the warmth with which you've welcomed me into your home; it is brimming with joy and love. Until next time, Trixie

Dear Mom and Dad,

Thanks again for these lovely days in Kimberley. The way you've welcomed Trix with open arms means a lot to me and I'm excited about some of the schemes in the works – You and Trixie's Emily Carr project, a potential family Christmas in Oman, Trix and my plan to start a new adventure in Europe, your and Dad's next move, sometime early next year. Though I'm happy to visit you anywhere, this place will always be special. Sending lots of love, Luke

And love to all, Trix, Mom, Dad, Andy, Ayla and Matt (miss you brother)

Tuesday, September 5, Bankastraat, The Hague, The Netherlands

Dear Terry Anne,

I write this as Joshua is in mid-air on his way to work on a one-month project in Kediri fostering inter-faith understanding. He will be stationed in an Islamic boarding school, living with a family and writing about his experiences for the British Council and British Embassy. Sam is in Geneva, visiting a Dutch friend – who he roomed with at Berkeley during his semester abroad – and is close to getting his entrepreneur's grant that will take him back to Berlin in November. Both appear to have used these few unexpected months living 'at home' as a family as a time to recalibrate. It seems they have many friends in the same boat at their age – mid-twenties. As your boys take the time in your Kimberley 'home base' to stop for a while, to have fun and to be mindful of what matters, I fully appreciate the value of providing a home for our ATCKs and am filled with guilt for not having done that for ours.

I wonder whether providing a home, a haven, a sanctuary, a safe place to fall, for kids like ours helps them to recover from the anxiety so many suffer from these days? I wonder if it helps them to cope with The Void that Joshua has talked of recently – this grey cloud that appears to hang over their age-group; a fear of a bleak future; a personal inability to achieve all they have been led to believe they are capable of? Into this mix I am pretty sure our ATCKs have a fair amount of unresolved grief, of loss in so many ways and I wonder how Luke, Matt and Andrew will feel going back to Oman?

There is no doubt that coming back to The Hague has been a good thing on so many levels. To some extent we all belong here and have a community. We know how things work. We have already acquired the skill of 'natural navigation' that is required by divers – we know where we are in relation to things we recognise. I find it soothing and expect they do too. We have never taken the boys back to Oman, but I have been back twice. I adore the fillip of recognising the familiar sights, smells, tastes and sounds. We've all been back to Dubai and though the boys were only one and two when we left, they had some sense of recognition. But for me, I only have to enter that infernal queue at passport control and I start to smile. No, I lie. The thrill begins from the moment the plane heaves into its turn and descent that I crane to drink in every scrap of the view. And then that smell on leaving the terminal. I think it is a mix of dry ice and raw chicken mixed with musky perfume. Believe me, I have spent a long time trying to find a way of describing it and each time I return I check my description again and it still holds.

But going back to Norway? A different experience altogether. I hated Stavanger. I was depressed in Stavanger. It seemed never to stop raining and I have no recollection of ever seeing blue sky. We picked the wrong house (yes, how your Doha story resonated) but did not move. We got burgled in the first few weeks. Sam started to show signs of unhappiness then. He was four, going on five and I expect his mood fed off mine. After years of never even wearing socks he now had to wear several layers of clothes, snowsuits topped with rainsuits and fur-lined wellies. I will never forget seeing him alone in the playground at break time. He wore his yellow snowsuit, zip down because he dared not zip it up in case he never got out again. He looked so sorrowful. I used to say that I felt like the loneliest pine tree in the forest – you know, surrounded by others who looked like me. One day as I waited in a throng of mums outside the front door to fetch Sam from school my only friend, Karen, turned to me and told me she was not surprised I was struggling to connect with people.

"You never look anyone in the eyes, you know, Jo?" she said.

I was mortified but that cruel-to-be-kind message was just what I needed to hear. Karen is still one of my dearest friends.

I share this because it was thanks to you that I did, eventually, return to Stavanger. It was four or so years ago and it was June when I visited you in your home. This time I was mortified once more. Not because anyone accused me of anything antisocial but because it was gorgeous. I found myself blindsided by how guilty I felt for not appreciating the place when we lived there, how my attitude formed my perception and stopped me from enjoying myself. I realised how important a positive mental attitude is but also that we manage expectations before we get to a place.

I wrote a poem called *Stavanger, I am Sorry*. It went like this:

Stavanger, I am Sorry

Stavanger, I am sorry
I never felt your sun,
nor saw the way it licked the rooves
and white-washed walls
until they shone like stars.

I'm sorry that I never heard
the scalloped fjords
scuff their shores
while in silence they would sigh and stretch
until their fingertips touched land.

My bones ache with regret
that my veiled eyes
were blinded then by memories —

of brighter sun, a warmer shore, a bluer sky —
so strong, like clouds, they hid your technicolour beauty.

To me, back then,
younger and more foolish,
my jaw was clenched against sweet sentences,
eyes narrowed into bitter slits
that refused to see the light,
as a toddler's tantrum lingers, though the ball's now in his hands.

It's fifteen years since I gladly waved goodbye
to a cold, damp year
that had left my soul screaming for sustenance
while a groaning table
had lain there all along.
I had never looked beyond the window
of my home-made prison.

Today, renewed and wiser,
I see the gift of blossom
that's lingering in June,
of clematis thick with pastels
and white peonies with a thicker scent
than I have ever known
and so I must record these thoughts —
and drag my eyes from waving trees, plump lambs
that trot on tussocked hills strewn

with rocks painted in lichen's rich Tuscan hues, the
buttercupped fields, the dips
and folds, the soaring fells that cluster
shoulder to shoulder round the fjords –
but I cannot bear to tear my eyes
from this, down to the page, lest
I miss a morsel of this Norwegian feast.

I recorded myself reciting this, leaning against a dry stone wall, against the most exquisite backdrop, on the island of Egerøy, south of Stavanger. You can still find it on YouTube.

And so, going back is something I think of often. I will be intrigued to learn how it affects you all.

We have just returned from a week-long holiday in a large French villa in the Dordogne with two other families we have known for 23 years, since we lived in Oman together, funnily enough. Joshua realised that these people were there at the seminal moments in each other's lives: like when he developed his fear of spiders, grandparents passed away or we moved on again. They have visited us in every country we moved onto and we have holidayed together countless times. In many ways, they are like family to us.

It was while we were away that Sam and Joshua requested a family meeting. We sat on two two-seater sofas facing each other in the manor's cavernous stone-flagged, stone-clad sitting room. Our body language spoke volumes. Ian was twisted sideways and kept clearing his throat. I leaned forwards. Sam leaned back and Joshua waved his arms about a lot, as if trying to ensure we were all fully engaged. I knew we were going to talk about retirement housing, which was why I leaned in. It's a topic I am desperate to resolve. Sam, I think, was nervous of the outcome. Joshua hopeful. Ian, worried.

"Sam and I feel very insecure at the moment," Joshua began.

"It's very unsettling the way you two keep discussing buying houses here, there and everywhere all the time, yet never do anything about it," said Sam.

"We need a base that is not going to change," they told us. "And we think it should be Stamford because Granny and Grandpa are there and need us and we all lived there for a while so it's the closest we have to any roots anywhere. And it's beautiful."

Sam would prefer it was London or somewhere a bit more edgy than the fine medieval stone town on the edge of Rutland and Lincolnshire where I grew up, but accepts Stamford makes sense. "I want to live somewhere where I can understand the conversations going on around me. I want things to be easier," he said.

"And I want us to put family first and be there for your parents, Mum," Joshua continued, so influenced by his time in the collective society of Java. "I could not bear for them to be in a home."

Ian and I have discussed the fact that I too am sick of moving now. I want to stay put and put down roots. I too

"Ultimately, work out why you are doing this journey of discovery. Have a clear purpose, set realistic goals, monitor and review these as a family. What about the future? Do you have a long term plan? When will you repatriate back home?"

Ian Moody

want to be there for my parents and I am prepared for him to travel to work and come home weekends.

Ian continued to clear his throat and stalled as much as he could get away with. "But first we need to get our Dutch house valued," he repeated again and again. He is such a serial thinker, which I find so frustrating. But in fact, we were all in agreement and the boys were mightily relieved.

Once back home, on Sunday evening I got a WhatsApp from my mother.

I've emailed you, it said.

I opened my email with trepidation. The email was titled *About Pa*.

In short, he has been getting lost in his own bedroom at night and very frightened and confused. She had kept all this from me so it did not spoil my holiday but she was taking my father to the doctor the next day. Yesterday.

He had blood tests and a memory test, which was terrible, apparently. He could not count back from 20, nor do the months of the year in reverse order. He now has to go and have a brain scan.

"It is very likely the start of dementia," said Dr Williams to my mother within Pa's earshot. Pa did not flinch and did not mention it again. My mother is in bits. I am flying home on Monday.

My brother and I have agreed that we will each visit them monthly so that they get a visit once a fortnight from one or other of us and we will phone more often. WhatsApp is all very well but it's not the same as a phone call or a Skype, is it? In the car on our way back from France we listened to Sheryl Sandberg on *Desert Island Discs* as she discussed her grief after the death of her husband. She advised that people ask those in crisis not how they are but 'how they are today'. This morning I WhatsApped my mother to ask how her night went.

I feel as if I am stepping into a new era. One where I have to be a support for my mother. I feel that I am donning a protective carapace and moving into practical mode. I think this is my coping mechanism and that organising and doing and fixing are much easier than facing the truth and the grief that is inevitable as my wonderful father slips away. I have to be strong for the kids who have never lost anyone close and for my mother who hates being in charge. I'm starting to set several plates spinning. For my parents, the boys, Ian, the house-hunt, my business and trying to re-establish a social life. Wish me luck!

While I was away I read somewhere that between an ending and a new beginning we must expect 'hurting time'. I guess this is felt particularly acutely by people like us. Then, yesterday, I saw a post on Facebook about grief that said the process is *Understand, Recognise, Touch, Move.*

We need to *Understand* there is no right way to grieve and everyone is different in how they cope with it. It may not show on the outside like a broken leg would do, but the pain is no less acute.

Then we should *Recognise* that we need to grieve and that it cannot be avoided.

Thirdly, we need to really *Touch*, or feel our grief, the anger, sadness, bitterness or whatever before *Moving* to the epicentre of our grief, which is where it will hurt the most, but it is only by experiencing the greatest sadness that we can move to a happier place again.

When I was in KL I saw an energy healer called Ian Yap. In our first meeting I found myself sharing about my childhood abuse. Ian made me sit with my emotion and I found myself shaking from head to toe, uncontrollably, for what felt like 15 minutes. He told me to hold the thought and really feel all the anger and fear and disgust and resentment. Once it was over I felt cleansed. I felt whole again. Six months later I feel free of that pain. Pain I had carried for half a century.

I recognise that it will be my turn to grieve and that I must give myself permission to be emotional. I don't want to bottle it up for years because I can't bear to face it, because I know that rather like a gas leak it will leak out of me anyway and poison the atmosphere. I hope I can help my mother usefully. I'm finding it hard to sleep again, worry too much and jump every time the phone rings. I bury myself in work. I bury my head in the sand. As usual I can see that I am eating more biscuits and bread, drinking that extra glass of wine and getting out in the fresh air less. As for meditating. It seems the more I know I should do all these things that make me feel better, the less I can motivate myself to do them. The 10 minutes of yoga I was doing in the morning has fallen by the wayside. Morning pages? Nope. Seems I have dropped those too.

So much seems to have happened since our last communication, both physically and in our heads. I used to call this the Expat Rollercoaster. No wonder it can be so exhausting!

With love,

Jo

Monday, September 11, Kimberley, British Columbia, Canada

Dearest Jo,

With the sad news of your father, and the implications for you all, I'm so sorry to hear this update. You described grief so well and the permission to grieve in its various stages. Please be sure to listen to that advice as you all move forward and as you juggle those difficult plates. Ah, how nice it would be to just sit and chat in person, yet all I can do now is let you know I'm thinking of you. But as is the usual with our meandering messages, there is good news, so great to hear of Joshua and his new venture to Indonesia. And Sam so close to getting an Erasmus grant to be in Berlin. In our communication since May, I marvel at the steps they've both taken forward in that short space of time. For our Andrew's sake, I only wish his journey had taken less time than it did. I promised to write of it. It is heartbreaking and inspiring, and I was proud when he agreed I could share it. I've put it off… it's time to share it.

We never expected Andrew to hit rock bottom or feel there wasn't a way forward. But perhaps that's what happened, and what finally prompted him to change his life. A few weeks ago, as he, Ayla, myself and Bruce cozied around a campfire, we played a game of 'conversation starter'. Andrew drew the card that asked, "What are you most thankful for in life?" He sat quietly and contemplated. There was a long pause, then the newly-turned 22-year-old chose his words very carefully.

"I am thankful for my family, you supported me through everything. I'm thankful that you guys and Ayla's parents have given us your support and love. And I'm actually thankful for everything I've gone through. The foundation you've given me, Mom and Dad, and all the pain and experiences, have given me the tools I need to succeed in life. I have it all now." Yet, it has been a journey.

Andrew was eight years old when he was catapulted from a 'perfect life' at a private British School in Oman, to a 'regular public' school in Katy, Texas. But not before the confusion of initially trying the British School in Houston. The details don't matter now, but what does are the cultural adjustments; in the end we stuck with the American system. School uniform traded for jeans and t-shirt, a bike-ride to school instead of an hour bus journey each way. The growing hint of a Texan twang, instead of a touch of a British accent. A dabble with 'footie' and cricket, replaced by hockey and baseball. And Andrew was a natural as we had suspected previously when Bruce and I had started a Little League when we lived in Oman. Within two months of moving to Katy, he was sought after by a travel team and chosen for an All-Star team. By the time he was 12 he was hitting so many home-runs, other parents would bring the keepsake balls to us that he had dinged over the fence – we had stopped collecting them as the pile at home grew.

When Andrew was 14 we announced that we were moving to Norway. At the end of the season just before we moved, yet another of his home-run hits sailed over the fence. His coach looked toward the stands and hollered for all to hear, "If y'all take this kid out of the US, you'll regret it forever."

We did take him away and we'll never know. And, yes, it has crossed his lips many times, "What if, what if we'd stayed?" Yet there he was now in Norway, in a small International school. Baseball was traded for rugby, basketball, football, even a stint with a Norwegian hockey team. There were trips throughout Europe, not only for sports but for Model United Nations, for French Immersion and for fun. With good friends and solid marks with an International Baccalaureate Diploma, the world was on his doorstep when he graduated. But first he had to say goodbye to his first true love, they had no choice but to part, and then to his many friends. Unlike most of them, whose parents were remaining in Norway, or indeed were from there, our posting was finished.

"Andrew," I remember suggesting, "you can go to university anywhere you choose. Maybe the UK where many of your friends will be?"

"No, Mom, it's time I become Canadian. I want to study in Canada."

He had never lived in his 'homeland', and those words would come to haunt me.

With a handful of acceptance letters, at the last-minute Andrew chose a smaller university on Vancouver Island in Victoria, rather than Vancouver. I wonder if things might have been different if he'd gone with the more international UBC from the outset. An incident a week before he set off foreshadowed what was to come. I was at our house in the mountains, he in that condo I had newly rented in Calgary. That was the year I had decided to spend some time at home instead of immediately joining Bruce in Kazakhstan. Opening my messages that morning, one from Andrew screamed out at me. "Mom, this is me. I have no home!" Attached was a blog he had found, written from an adult TCK... *"Don't ask me where I'm from, don't ask me where home is."*

Knowing my son needed someone to talk to, I made my way back to the city. That evening we started a game of Scrabble, and we didn't get past the second turn.

"Mom, I've had to give up everything. My sports, my friends, my girlfriend. This life sucks. Dad is half-way around the world and you really should be there with him. And now where do I even say I'm from? How is this suddenly supposed to be home?"

I understood it perfectly; I didn't know what I was doing either. My mostly charmed expat life was suddenly on hold. I was living away from my husband. I had some friends in the city, my parents a few hours away and it was lovely that Luke was living with me while on a gap year before starting a Master's, but even I spent some days feeling bewildered. I was going back and forth from our place in the mountains to the condo. I was crying on Luke's shoulder, missing my husband, worrying about Matt and the start of his descent into his reclusiveness.

Suddenly my struggles were extraneous. I counselled Andrew for hours.

"You're a TCK, of course," I began.

"Mom, I know about this third culture label, but what good does it do me? All I know is that the great life I had is gone. I'm going where I know no one. Am I supposed to just forget that life ever happened?"

"Andrew, that needs to be part of your identity, it's your past, who you are. Those experiences make you unique and now you get to be in your home country. You have to try to embrace that." I'm sure deep down I knew it would not be as easy as I was trying to make it sound.

I know now that those first months on campus set the tone. As is the reality of university, not only do our kids leave the comfort and support of a home and family, they have to adjust to life in a postage-stamp sized residence, and find a new tribe. For Andrew, people couldn't get past the fact he had lived in Norway and beyond. What was once the norm of a global life, was now an anomaly. He was different, apparently the 'privileged' kid, and began telling white lies to avoid the long form of his story. Anything to avoid judgement and the preconceptions of having lived out of Canada. He quickly traded his Euro-style clothing for jeans and a t-shirt, a baseball cap to finish it off. "Clothes are always a coping mechanism," he admitted recently, "I curated my style to blend in as much as possible."

"The main difference for ATCKs is that the impact of mobility, interrupted friendships and educations, unresolved grief and other common experiences of TCK Childhood, compound some of the challenges during emerging adulthood."

Ellen Mahoney

That first Christmas home he seemed a little subdued and we talked; he assured me he was fine. At Easter, he flew home again and maybe I was so delighted to have all three boys under one roof that I missed any signs of distress. Final exams were pending, nothing seemed out of the ordinary.

At the end of the school year, Andrew came home for what I thought would be for summer break. "Mom you should maybe sit down," he said a few weeks later. Final marks were in.

"I'll just come out with it, I've failed. In fact, I've failed so badly I've been kicked out. University is over. I own it. It's my fault." He let it sink in. "And I've decided, I'm joining the army – Infantry." I knew that meant a foot soldier.

There weren't enough words to describe my shock, my disbelief and then my dismay. My gregarious, athletic, smart, well-travelled son was going to be a soldier?!

Images of his high-school graduation in Norway replayed in my mind. *Please can we just rewind and go back,* a voice inside me screamed. Back to the graduation ceremony... Andrew strolling across the stage, face beaming as he accepted his IB diploma with credits for University and the award for Sportsman of the Year. Back to that brilliant grad party we had held in our garden with a massive Arabic tent as the backdrop... oh joy, good friends still happened to have one from the good ol' days of camping in Qatar. Back to those kids and parents from around the world, deliriously proud after four years of high school and reaching this milestone. The future seemingly as bright as the Northern Lights that faithfully illuminate the skies of that beautiful country. *Please, please can we go back to that time and start over...*

But you can't and the Skype call to Kazakhstan to break the news to his father was one I could not have envisioned. More disbelief. But as always, Bruce was stoic, or attempted to be. A month or so later I drove Andrew to the Canadian Armed Forces Recruiting Offices in Calgary. I was proud of his resolve, but did I really want him to be successful in his application? I pre-empt this by clarifying how much respect I have for the Military and know that it is a chosen path for many. And I now understand that it is not just the person who is called to duty, it is the entire family in one form or another – the worry and the sacrifice to begin with.

As Andrew waited for acceptance, he returned to Victoria where he lived with friends. His social circle is large and as they all got back to school life, Andrew mostly holed up in his room in a grungy basement suite. He partied, he played video games, he worked part-time... he waited.

By then I had joined Bruce in Kazakhstan, Luke was now in Sweden starting his Master's degree, Matt in Calgary back in university part-time… a family once again scattered to the proverbial four corners.

It was early morning in our Aktau hotel suite when we heard the news. The suite looked out to the Caspian Sea and we had chosen it rather than moving into a house. We loved it and we were happily together again, but worried constantly about Matt, and now about Andrew. The message came just after I had woken up. Bruce walked gingerly over to the bed and took my hand in his hand.

"Sweetheart, he's in. He's in the Army." The cry rose from the pit of my stomach, like a wave, unstoppable and mournful to its core. I cried like I had never in my life, rocking back and forth, back and forth in my husband's arms. I still cry, every time I think or speak of that moment. Yes, I've cried writing of it... a wound etched on my heart.

Less than two weeks later, we're on the convoluted journey to Victoria to give him a proper farewell, to be at the ceremony as he's sworn in. "You understand you may be put in harm's way, that death can be a consequence of this job?" the new recruits are asked solemnly. At least I think it was something like that, because later as we sat with 20 or so of Andrew's friends at his 'going away' dinner I realised I couldn't quite put all the pieces together. And now this setting seemed too convivial. His friends loved him and were so very proud of his decision. They'd miss him, but he could always come back when he had a break.

Then an early morning flight arranged by the army, and he was gone. Thirteen weeks of boot camp, of re-wiring, of strict discipline, he'd later say. Bruce and I stayed a week longer and fled to Tofino, to the ocean. We kayaked and cried, cried and kayaked some more. Bruce's father had been Military, SAS, in his younger days and Andrew had always been intrigued. We shouldn't be that surprised we told ourselves. We'd both be fine, then one of us would mention it and it would start all over again; oscillating between acceptance and pride, then to denial and guilt. It was our fault, we rationalised. If that job had materialised in Calgary after Houston like it was supposed to have done, rather than Norway, this wouldn't be happening. He would have had a hometown. He would have felt Canadian and not struggled with his identity, and then university.

Yet here he was stepping up and serving his country, as a Canadian. We were being incredibly selfish. Brave young men and women serve and we need these military people and their supportive families. Finally, we managed to stop the tears and, as you mention Jo, grieve. We needed that time alone in a serene setting to come to terms with how things once had been and how they now were. It was grieving in some form. And it was finally finding the strength to move forward and support our son.

PART 2

The phone calls usually came about 6am, just as Bruce was getting ready for work. Never, ever, did he sleep without his phone on his bedside table. Andrew might be calling from Basic Training. It was somewhere close to Montreal and calls were occasionally allowed. *Yup, just calling my mom and dad in Kazakhstan.* As usual, our son is the odd man out. "Why are your parents in Kazakhstan?" the officials had wanted to know. "What kind of work is your dad in?" Yes, I think we might have had a background check done on us.

Initially we would take Andrew's calls together. We'd gauge his voice, his tone, things he was saying or not saying. It was difficult, but he told us that his athleticism helped. They were always sleep deprived. They'd had a few outings on the weekends. Pretty cool wearing that uniform, you got respect. He and his new buddies had worked a system, someone shined the boots, someone sewed the badges or whatever had to be done; teamwork. He admitted his platoon usually slept on top of their beds in order to save precious time in the morning, more time to ensure things were in place for inspection. Things had to be exact – military precision. But he understood why this was important, why they were being done this way.

By week seven or so, I often wouldn't rouse for the calls. Bruce would take meticulous notes of the conversation and leave them for when I woke up. Each word precious, and I remember this note clearly… *Tomorrow we get our guns, one more thing to worry about.*

Then we knew he was leaving for his week-long deployment in the field, where training intensified, where live ammunition was used and where things start to feel very real. They were in the wilderness in simulated combat situations, under tense and challenging circumstances. A picture was taken of him in full combat gear, face camouflaged, with his rifle at his side, seemingly at one with the forest behind him. I can describe it, as I'm looking at it as I write. Not long ago it was displayed on his desk, but today I had to dig for it. It was tucked away in one of his drawers along with his Certificate – the one announcing he had passed Basic Training and was now officially in the Army.

Thirteen weeks later, at the end of training, we once again flew from Kazakhstan to Canada for the graduation and military parade. Hundreds of parents, siblings and grandparents sat on bleachers inside a massive hangar. From all over Canada, and a few from around the world, we had come to witness this proud moment. Some were exuberant and proud, others fought back tears, a few wept openly. Afterwards we had dinner with two other families – the kids were buddies, though one was somewhat older and they were now each going their separate ways. Andrew, and another friend, had chosen to be Infantry soldiers; "To start at the bottom," Andrew had told me. As I sat at this 'last supper', there was talk from one of the new soldiers of forays to strip clubs in Montreal, of other exploits I would rather not have known. I couldn't process the conversation, nor the situation. I looked across the table at my 20-year-old, trying to stay composed. I had exactly four more hours with my son. He had to be back at base camp at 21:00 hours and at 0:500 hours he was being transferred to another training facility. We had no idea when we would see him again, none.

Andrew looked back at me with concern, with love. He knew me well; I'm sure he knew I couldn't bear the thought of not knowing when we'd see each other again. I was reliving the moments of a mother and her son, of our strong, loving bond.

When I trailed behind his golden curls as he rode round and round on his tricycle… me and the cat chasing the tin can he was pulling behind his prized 'vehicle,' laughter ringing through our Doha garden.

When I helped him dig tiny graves in our Omani garden, for the baby birds that our dog Mojo seemed unable to resist. "Mommy, let's say something for the birds," he'd say, before reprimanding our playful black-and-white springer spaniel.

When we moved to Houston, the first time, and he was too young for kindergarten in the US and was home again. He insisted we set up an easel and have 'art class' in what became our open-air 'studio' on the balcony. Magical is the word that comes to mind. He was my baby and I suddenly had another year with him, just the two of us.

Or when I'd been his baseball coach, and then happily 'turned him over to the experts' though still scored hundreds of his games as he played in Houston and beyond. It was our thing: glorious, long evenings at the ballpark.

And when he'd been all that helped keep me together when just the three of us moved to Norway. Though he was suddenly an 'only' child, he cracked jokes to help ease the pain when I burst into tears over and over again – our table was used to a family of five.

And then that last year in Norway when he came downstairs and asked if his girlfriend could stay the night. Sex, respect and protection had to be discussed. Yes, his dad also discussed this with him, but always, always I felt we could talk about everything and anything. We had each other's back.

Back at the hotel, we count down the last two hours of this final taste of freedom before Battle School. Once you've started the training, the commitment is three years. Now, he no longer has the strength to stay awake.

"Sorry, Mom and Dad, I just need to sleep for a few minutes. We trained non-stop for weeks for the parade. I'm just so, so tired."

He takes off his 'dog tag' and puts it on the bedside table. I will never forget picking it up and seeing its two identical pieces – one that stays with the body, the other finds its way to the family. I caress it as if it is him, wanting to protect my son and take away any pain – now, or what the future may bring. I sit on the bed beside my boy and stroke his hair but the curls are long gone. Now it's just the bristly edges of his army cut.

I need a long hug from Bruce and then we just sit. We wait and let him sleep as long as we can, but it's almost 21:00 hours and time for our farewell. We watch him salute and march back into the building… the image truly speaks for itself, it's too difficult to write.

One month later, I'm in the Netherlands with my mother and then we head to Spain to stay with family on the coast. In Alicante, I see wave after wave of young people. They're Andrew's age, out and about enjoying tapas and drinks, chatting and laughing. I know Andrew was here a few years ago with his friends doing just this, being young and free, and I still cannot reconcile it. I cannot seem to accept that he's in a barrack waiting for a future that I know he was brave enough to have chosen, but did he truly want it?

And then the message from Bruce. *You must call me, as soon as you can, it's Andrew.*

Andrew's words were that he needed our blessing. He had made a mistake. He'd become disillusioned with military life, he'd decided it wasn't his future after all. He worried of the challenge of maintaining a relationship, a family, the feeling of a lack of control over his life. He wasn't a quitter, but this was his last chance. And despite the stigma of leaving, he'd seen an opening as the start of Battle School had been delayed – he wanted our blessing to leave, while he still could. Both Bruce and I said yes, there was no hesitation. I understand how this can be perceived by those who have a loved one in the military. I simply don't know how to respond to that. I do know that when he was asked why he was making the decision, his answer was that he didn't like the person he was becoming. I don't know what else to say. I just know that I wanted what was best for my son.

When we welcomed him home that September, he stood in the kitchen of our home and looked around as if seeing it for the first time. "You don't know how many times I dreamed of just standing here, of just being home."

He was a changed person. We listened, we counselled, we hugged often. We had five precious days together before we all 'deployed' back to our respective parts of the world. The future was unclear, but thankfully he had friends to reunite with in Victoria. Now in their third year of university, he did his best to fall back into step, but of course it wasn't the same. Some volunteer experience, a summer job at Starbucks, one year failed at university, less than a year in the Canadian Military – good enough to get a job as a line cook at a restaurant. Then it was Christmas and when he came home, thankfully it was just the two of us before the others arrived.

A three-hour conversation – this one would direct the next part of his journey.

"Mom, what happened to my life?" Andrew said, failing to fight back the tears. "Look at me, I feel like an old man. I had a beautiful life, around smart friends, with futures. I'm working in a low-skilled job. I'm sure they're good people, but it's not me. How am I here?"

"But parents might want to prepare for – and not be hurt – when their older children let them know in no uncertain terms that the lifestyle of constant change is not what they want for themselves."

Becky Grappo

We cried. We went back and forth, around and around for hours and hours. How things could have been different; what could we have done better? And then I knew, the past had to be the past.

"Andrew that's it, enough. Take what you've learned, the strength and the experiences you've gained. You have to go forward. And, son, you know what? You can go back to university. Start again, we will still support you, in a heartbeat."

He looked me and it's as if a thousand-pound weight drifted away from his broad shoulders. "I can, can't I? Mom, I think I will."

"Come on, let's get to bed. That's enough for one night," I said through tears as he hugged me good night.

The next morning after turning on the Christmas tree lights and peeking out to another snowfall on our tall pines, I heard a 'good morning' from Andrew's room. It was early. Already at his desk, he was applying for universities. We looked at each other and nodded knowingly. I'm sure tears filled my eyes – it was the only Christmas present I needed.

Three months later, he was accepted into UBC, for the second time. He's convinced it was the impassioned letter that accompanied his application. A university in Sweden also beckoned, but Andrew was steadfast: "I have to make a new start for myself; Vancouver is where I'm calling home. I'm not going anywhere." He made the right decision.

Last week, I watched as he and Ayla took down their tent after our night in the great outdoors. They worked in unison, happy as a team. They delighted in the new camping lantern we'd given Andrew for his birthday; it already had a place of its own in their 'camping box' – they're organised to a tee. And they're in love and in love with life and all the good possibilities before them. Ayla is a scientist in the making and my dear Andrew? Well, he's a former athlete and soldier. He's a lifeguard, a manager who handled two painting crews this past summer. He's a 'mature student'.

"It's a bit different this time, Mom," he told me. "My views are different. I know the importance of this degree, I'm not going to get a third chance." He's an all-round good guy; one that needed more time, support and understanding, but he got it right.

"Andrew, can I write your story?" I asked as we said goodbye last week. "Yes, do, Mom, maybe it can help other kids and parents from going through what I did. Perhaps the school could have prepared us better as TCKs, I'm not sure. I had no idea how difficult it would be to adjust, to find my identity. In the end, maybe I had to find out the hard way and grow from it. Hey, it's all good. Love you guys!"

And off he and Ayla went, ready for the ten-hour drive to Vancouver where a place was waiting for them to move into – close to the beach and perfectly placed between their respective universities. I couldn't smile or wave happily enough!

Love for now, Jo,

Terry Anne

Monday, September 18, Bankastraat, The Hague, The Netherlands

Dear Terry Anne,

I was stunned to read your story about Andrew. I may have been your friend for five years now but it is unbelievable that so much of what you shared I did not know. Sure, I knew about the army and knew about his search for the right path, but there was so much more. It is clear that only by writing proper letters like this do we allow ourselves to truly open our hearts and tell the whole story to each other. Wouldn't you agree? I knew you were an emotional person because I have seen your eyes fill with tears a few times. But, maybe it's because of that inherited Dutch resilience of yours that I had no idea quite how devastated you were by Andrew's story. I suppose the reason I notice this is because in your last email you obeyed one of the first rules of writing story – that of Show Not Tell. You showed me how and where and how often you cried. You showed me how supportive Bruce is, always. How, despite spending time in the nature that you so love, your heartbreak remained.

Writing to you over these last few months – would you believe it is now almost six months? – I realise that we have opened up to each other in a deeper way than I often do to my very dearest, very oldest friends. Maybe it is because when we write, rather than speak, there is no ping of a phone to distract us, no time limit and the conversation does not flow back and forth – with one of us chipping in and sharing our own story, or nodding, or offering affirmation and support.

I remember once that a friend of mine was in therapy and she told me how her counsellor just sat there and let her speak. It did not matter how long the silence went on for. He did not prompt. He just waited. And then once my friend began to speak, he waited again for her to finish, and simply said something like, "go on," and thus she was encouraged to talk herself dry. In these emails we can 'write ourselves dry' too. I think that is so important.

As I write this you must be heading to India. I wonder how it will be to be back and how you will find Matt when you arrive. You will be pleased to know (I know we are) that Sam definitely got his Erasmus Young Entrepreneur's grant and will head to Berlin in six weeks for six months. Joshua is just back from Indonesia, where he has been in his happy place. I am here, finding it hard to get used to the cold after all that time in Malaysia as I wait for our small shipment from the UK to arrive and with it, at last, our kitchen bin and vacuum cleaner! It has been a year now since we entered the limbo of not knowing when or where we would be moving as Ian applied for jobs within the company. It feels like we have lost or even wasted that year with having four different places to call home, wondering what will happen, worrying about family and being unsettled. But, despite it all, I have retained and even grown my business, adding retreats to the mix, I have had a few holidays and dinner parties and, most

"Of course, there are times when we do not want to be in limbo. We wonder why can't we just settle down and have the routine like others. But this is not the case. So learning to be in the state of limbo means adjusting ourselves to live in the 'grey' and not the defined black and white."

Lesley Lewis

importantly, I have laughed. I am, however, officially sick of moving!

This week I went back to England for the I-don't-know-how-manyth time this year. Maybe the seventh? Tomorrow marks the day that we have been 'back' in The Hague for six months. Time has flown and frighteningly we may now be a quarter of the way through this posting. Anyway, I flew back to stay with my parents and give my mother the support she needed. She doesn't like to disturb me because I "have enough to worry about" without her piling her problems on. I wish I could persuade her to let us have a chat every day on the phone so she can let off steam and vent her frustrations but she is too worried Pa will listen in and she does not want to upset him further.

I really am worn out from all those ten-hour drives home, so this time I flew to Luton airport and hired a car, which meant I arrived in better shape.

"Look, I'm still alive!" he announced when I arrived. It was past their bedtime and they were both in dressing gowns and slippers waiting up for me.

"I can see that, Pa!" I replied, giving him a big hug and a kiss, relieved he still has his sense of humour.

"Hello, Bizzy! Me again." I greeted my mother with hugs and kisses and can sense her emotion as usual. Tears are always near the surface whenever she hugs anyone arriving or leaving. They always are. I had not told you that I have never called my mother 'Mum'. In my teens, I moved straight from calling her 'Mummy' to 'Bizzy'. It's a long story involving a chiropodist called Mr Biggs and a poem my school friend wrote about a dragon and soon became the perfect nickname for my permanently 'busy' mother. Flower club, church flowers, voluntary work with the food bank and Meals on Wheels, art club, coffee with her friends, waiting on my father hand and foot. One of the biggest impacts of my father's ageing has been the guilt she feels at leaving him so she can go out and do her usual activities.

"He hates me going out," she says with a mix of sorrow and resentment. "I'm going to have to give up doing my things." *My life*, I could hear written between the lines. I don't want that and I am sure neither does Pa.

My mother is so like me. Defined and boosted by the activities she takes part in and her important friendships. For as long as I can remember they have had drinks with friends and neighbours at 6pm on a Friday and met others in the pub for a meal. Now that my father is 90 all, literally all, of his friends have passed away. Chatting about his passions for cars, aeroplanes, jazz, theatre, books and travel was his greatest joy. He was always known for his incredible optimism and enthusiasm for life. Until very recently he was still writing articles for the parish magazine. He was the person responsible for putting the first computer in Peterborough Technical College and was head of their computing until he took early retirement at 55, which is when his writing career began.

Now he struggles to open an email.

So, that's my parents. Both engaged, active and stimulated. Now, at 82 and 89, things have changed. I remember how, back in February, I met them halfway between England

and Kuala Lumpur for a holiday in Dubai. They thought the long-haul flight to KL would be too much and so for the first time in the 30 years of my expatriate life they were not coming to stay for three weeks. Our expatriate life had begun in Dubai and so being back there is always special.

The three of us lay side by side on comfortable loungers under an umbrella looking out at the Persian Gulf. The sand is long and flat, raked into perfect rows by some kind of tractor every morning. The sea is flat and calm, the palest aquamarine, low waves lick at the shore with a gentle transparent foam. Pa has forgotten to bring his reading glasses again and had already had a post-breakfast nap.

"I'm off for a wander," he declares and off he goes, stumbling slightly and just a little unsteady on the softly undulating sand. He refuses to surrender to a stick, though Bizzy and I wish he would give in. He gets angry if we try to take his arm. Rather than settle down to read our own books or gaze at the sea, we watch his progress down the beach.

"He'll never find us again," she says with resignation and draws me under her grey cloud of concern. He really is in amazing shape for 89 as, barefoot, he moves up and down the shoreline, paddling in the shallows, his hands clasped behind his back. Luckily he is wearing a straw trilby, which makes him easy to spot.

"Look, he's on his way back now." And she sits upright, over-empathising with the frustration he is bound to feel when he can't find our spot on the beach. As expected he overshoots and we watch him approach another row of three loungers with two occupied by women. "You'll have to go and rescue him," she says. And so I go.

Later he decides to return to the room for something and is gone an hour, lost. I find him looking confused in the lobby.

We join some good friends for dinner and Pa is overjoyed to discover that Mark loves to drive rally cars and digs into a deep and meaningful conversation that has him posting Mark the photocopy of an article later.

This is how it is for Bizzy and for me. Always looking for signs. Does he have dementia or doesn't he? We play Scrabble and he spells 'bought' B-O-R-T and time stands still as we all swallow our sudden panic. He calls the bank about a missing payment and we relax a little. He retreats upstairs to find a jumper and comes down wearing Bizzy's tee-shirt, gets angry, wrenches it back over his head and flings it down on the sofa. He goes to watch the movie Dunkirk alone and loves it. Has he or hasn't he? He spends longer and longer each day just sitting staring into space, even at the dining table. But he eats well and has a fabulous appetite.

But back to my recent trip. I wanted to give my mother the chance of a guilt-free few days of art and flowers and see if I could stimulate my father and help him regain the enthusiasm for which he has been so well known and so loved throughout his life. With his 90th birthday in a few weeks we looked through old photograph albums and I took notes. I can hardly believe it has been decades since I last looked at those pictures. Some I did not recognise at all, but in those pages I saw a man I had almost forgotten. There he was surrounded by lovely young girls, picnicking like in the Manet painting *Le Déjeuner sur l'herbe*.

"Quality time can be a visit for a week – stay for extended periods of time and do a range of activities that the elderly person enjoys... for me it is about quality time rather than how often."

Ian Moody

"Who are they?" I asked, chuffed to see that my old man had been quite a player in his time it seemed.

"One of them is my first girlfriend," he said, too coy to elaborate.

In those collapsing pages, the photo-corners no longer holding the crinkly-edged photographs in place, I saw my father on his European road trips with his school-friends – fully made-up as an old-man in *When We Are Married* or as a soldier in *Henry V.* There he was driving a rally car, being a Best Man, courting the rather gorgeous 21-year-old who became my mother. We spent a wonderful two hours down memory lane. There he was visiting us in Dubai, Oman, Norway, the Netherlands and Malaysia too. I took a gazillion photos of the images in preparation for the birthday book I will make him, and was so glad I had the opportunity to recognise not only the amazing life he led before I came on the scene, but the incredible opportunities our life abroad has given him – a chap who always loved to travel.

My mother is eight years his junior and expects that she will be the one left behind. But she never paid into the UK pension scheme and is scared she won't have enough income to stay on in the cottage they rent. My father can't remember whether she will get a portion of his current teacher's pension. Neither of them has any idea how much she will get from the state pension. She can't use Internet banking either and I realise that my role is now switching to that of parenting them. My brother and I are looking into taking out Power of Attorney for them but in the meantime, I know we must ensure all bank accounts are in joint names and not his alone.

I used this trip to find out a bit more about their financial circumstances, spend a couple of nights in the camp bed in Pa's study and let my mother talk to me in peace on the swing seat in the garden while Pa napped. I returned to The Hague feeling I'd done something vaguely useful, only to receive a phone call from my brother, Patrick.

"Bizzy is desperate for a break," he said. "I'd like to fetch her to come and stay for a bit but what about Pa?"

I could almost hear the spinning plates start crashing all around me. I was desperate to spend more than two weeks together here in our house without having to go anywhere, and sort out those mountains of boxes, and couldn't face going back there again already. It was high time I was there for Ian, who is working so hard that a hot home-cooked meal on the table every night is one of his only pleasures. I wanted to be there for Sam when he gets back from his night shifts and to give Joshua the time he needs to discuss his worries. I needed to get back to a routine with yoga classes and a social life. Oh and, of course, I always prioritise my client work and needed to fit in my usual workday on top of all this.

"I think I'm going to cancel my Penang Me-Treat," I said one day over supper.

"But it's what you have always wanted to do!" Joshua said. "How can you?"

"Can you get a refund on your flight?" asked Ian, ever practical.

"No, but that's not the point," I whined. "I just can't fit it all in. Something's got to give."

"I'll go and look after Grandpa," Joshua offered and so, he, bless him, has stepped into the breach and willingly so. "I did it before, and it was fine. I can do it again."

He has too and actually he likes it. Being back in England, in the only town he feels remotely able to call home, he finds some kind of peace, he tells me. He has bought a flat tweed cap and wears a sleeveless padded jacket and is able to blend in with the locals. Earlier in the year he was researching and writing that book on the local heritage trade of Collyweston slating, and had the good fortune to see the place he claims he loves from both up on a roof and down a mine, which really helped him to find his own story. When he is there he loves to walk past the school he used to attend and catch up with a few of his old mates, although he left that school when he was only 12. It's familiar. The old stone buildings are beautiful. The winding lanes and perfect Georgian squares are charming, the churches captivating. I know just how he feels. I spent the first 26 years of my life there and love it as much today as I did then. Like me, he appreciates what England has to offer and loves to take Pa to the pub for fish and chips and half a pint of real ale. Who can blame him? I was never in any doubt about my roots. It is not that easy for our TCKs. Joshua says his grandparents' home is incredibly important to him.

"Honestly, Mum, I'm happy to go. Granny needs a break. Besides. I love my granny and grandpa. They are my living roots. No one else in the world says, 'Bread and pull it!' when I ask what's for supper."

It seems my son is looking after my best interests. I have another trip pending, this time to Oslo to the 20th WIN Conference, and I need a break too. A proper one!

With love until the next time,

Jo x

Monday, September 25, Bangalore, India

Dear Jo,

I write from my desk in India. A monsoon rain has refreshed the lush canopy outside my windows; the greens now more vibrant, the delicate raintree more alive. For some reason, the bougainvillea on my terrace refuses to bloom ("Madam, you have three boy bougainvilleas," Priya says cheekily), but my wispy palms are prolific and full. And, yes, as per the instruction of my Jaipur astrologer, I'm donning white this cool, damp Monday morning in Bangalore. It really does feel good to be 'home.'

Jo, first I need to tell how your words moved me to tears. The poignant description of your father… what an interesting, vibrant man. You have already done him a great honour in your writing of him, his character captured so beautifully. And your dear Bizzy, a woman who as you say, has not ventured far from where she was born, except perhaps to visit her daughter and family. Now to be cherished by them, by her grandsons who are so mindful of this stage in her life and their grandfather's – do not doubt the sense of family you have all created for them. Is that not what we should all hope for? To enjoy the pleasures of hobbies and clubs, of good friends and belonging to a community – you captured it all beautifully.

I've been back for just over a week. I don't know about you, but without fail it seems to take me that long to transition back to this 'other life'. I usually keep to myself, adjusting to the change of scenery, to the slower pace and to the separation from the family I've left behind. Eventually I find my mental equilibrium, but inevitably my reality is that melancholy sets in. Yet, at the same time, I am also ready to be back. I've learned to accept this. I reconcile it and tell myself not to get frustrated, to have patience, that it will pass. Thankfully, after about a week, it usually does.

This past week however, I resolved that I needed 'help' and returned to the therapy of yoga. I've made a commitment (yes once again) to practice every other day. So far it has helped my mood. Like you, I seem more conscious of my physical health lately. India has given me plantar fasciitis and allergies (must be those perfect sidewalks and pristine air) and then there are the effects of jet lag and travel. This past week on one of my 'do nothing' days I decided to document my travel since we moved to Bangalore – thank goodness for photos and my blogs to keep it all straight! When I read the list I had jotted down, I was reminded of the planning, the packing, the jet lag, the layovers, the transition time – the sheer amount of energy it all takes.

And I was shocked. In one and a half years, the number of trips I've taken is frightening (and a sustainability nightmare Luke would remind me). Keeping in mind that many of these trips in and out of India involve two long-haul flights. I discovered I had travelled more than 30 times… India, the Netherlands, India, Malaysia, India, Borneo and Malaysia, India, Sweden and Denmark, India, Canada, India, Singapore and Australia, India, Malaysia, India, Canada, India, Singapore, India, Brunei, India, Thailand, India, the Netherlands, Canada, Wales, India. Again, I'm incredulous of this list even though I was the one doing the travelling; surely it couldn't have been that many flights?

Nonetheless, the list prompted me to do a bit of research about air travel. We all know the annoyance of jet lag, or the odd flu we attribute to picking up on a flight. But what I found is quite disturbing, and it seems our so-called 'jet-setting' life is doing us ample harm. The disruption of our circadian rhythm from jetlag affects mood, judgment and concentration – no wonder I'm usually a 'mess' for seven days or more. Yet there are more serious implications to so much air travel. Besides psychological and emotional, research points to the physiological: disruption of gene expression that influences ageing and the immune system, the increased risk of heart attacks, strokes, and deep vein thrombosis. And to top it off, I admit that I had no idea that we are subjected to cosmic radiation every time we fly. That adage 'ignorance is bliss' comes to mind!

In reality, I don't know what it means for our life as expats. Like many, we travel home to see family, then for business, often for pleasure. As an empty nester that's one of the bonuses… you get to hop on a plane when you decide to. No school schedules or tickets for five to pay for. But does this seem more troubling because we're no longer 30, or even 40 years old? I now understand when people just say, "No thanks, I'm not interested in flying." Sadly, this summer, a good friend of ours, the same age, passed away from multiple blood clots. Unbeknownst to him, they had made their way to various parts of his body. He had also travelled often for business, and his death has impacted us. I had a long talk with his lovely widow before I left Canada. She's a good friend and said something that really touched me: "You have to live each day to the fullest and you know, it's better that we don't know what's in front of us." I think of her often. She would give anything for time... just more time.

"We had done the hard work," she told me. Referring to her husband who had died so unexpectedly, she told me that they had raised the kids who are finally all doing well. "This was meant to be our time. We had our getaway... we had the rest of our lives in front of us."

It breaks my heart. And yet she knows she has to move forward and I'm thankful for her that she has a good base of friends in their adopted home of Houston. I think of her often and in fact it helped influence our decision this summer as to whether we were staying in our adopted hometown of Kimberley. Yes, we love it as I've written, but we yearned for something on the water, on the coast – perhaps Vancouver. Thinking of my friend and what she's going through, once and for all we stopped talking about it and made the decision. If we were to start all over again in a new location and if anything were to happen to either Bruce or myself, how would we ever cope without the friends and the history we already have in Kimberley? I just couldn't imagine it. And so the decision was made. End of story; we're not going anywhere. I have always found that when clarity presents itself, it has to be trusted. And I hope for the day sometime soon when I can give my friend the biggest of hugs.

Jo, again, this reminds me of your parents, of my parents, who have a solid community. More and more I see the importance and value of this. When you speak of finally having chosen where you will retire I am pleased, and relieved for you. I understand the 'shift' you mention in adjusting now that the decision is made, and I think I spoke of it in my message that I wrote from Jaipur. Something like, *At some point we have to commit to a decision, accept it, and grow gracefully into it.* And you will. And, yes, the launching of your dream, Writing Me-Treats are a wonderful part of your ongoing journey. A good friend said something poignant when I was home this time: "Terry Anne, stop thinking that when you come home it's the end of this great life you have. Start thinking of it as the beginning of something else really wonderful." I will try to live to that when we do eventually repatriate.

I say eventually as now it seems almost certain that it won't be Canada this next move; one more location will present itself before home does. We have a slight idea of the possibilities, but things will unfold over the next few months for a possible move in March. I find it ironic that I only now feel as if I've truly found my 'tribe'. I've joined a group of women, many of whom are Indian. It's given me the opportunity to be welcomed, often into their beautiful older villas, and to be embraced by their warmth and rich culture.

"As they say, use it or lose it and this applies to past and newly acquired hobbies/activities that mentally and physically stimulate us in an age appropriate way."

Ian Moody

Speakers are also welcomed and elaborate on an array of subjects, the life of Gandhi being one of the latest. Needless to say, Jo, I am in my element. In fact, I'll be speaking for them soon… yes, to the power of writing!

I'll enjoy these last months in India. No, most days I'm not ready to leave and there's trepidation of the next location. Yet the rest of the year will be busy with a visit from a dear friend, then off to Penang in November. And of course, the anticipation of all the 'kids' coming for Christmas and seven of us traipsing across parts of India – it will be a treasured time.

I'm pleased to hear the good news about Sam and Joshua. I nodded knowingly when you mentioned the joy of sharing and reliving old memories; these times become even more precious now. I also full-heartedly concur when you say you feel there's been a wasted year with the process of an overseas move – with months of where, then months of planning the how, then the execution of it all. What a tangled journey we live. Soon it seems, my turn for the process will begin all over again.

Speaking of journeys, it was a relief to finally write of that other journey, that of Andrew's. I knew it was a powerful story and now that it's a little easier for me to tell, perhaps finally without tears, I agree that opening up through writing has been very therapeutic. While I lived in Houston, a number of us aspiring writers started writing *Morning Pages*. The author Julia Cameron encouraged writing daily in her book *The Artist's Way* and I admit I didn't remain committed for very long. I now know why. I didn't truly appreciate the value of writing, the therapy and solace it provides. I didn't realise the balm it was for the soul and the satisfaction it gives to claim a journey or story as your own – forever committed to words.

In *The Right to Write*, Julia Cameron wrote, "We should write because it is human nature to write. Writing claims our world. It makes it directly and specifically our own [...] We should write because writing is good for the soul."

We have certainly done that over the past six months, Jo, and it's been an awakening. Not only deepening our conversations and highlighting myriad issues, it has helped establish a few other truths for me: how a good commitment becomes habit-forming and also the importance of consistency. There is going to be a gaping hole once we no longer pen these 'letters' every Monday. It's been such a joy – yes, even writing through the tough stuff. I recall how it all started with a thought… what if we were to do this?

And I muse how many 'ifs' have brought me to this place. Finding my path as an empty nester has been a journey of learning and growth, of fulfilment and achievement, despite the challenges. What if I hadn't ventured to your writer's retreat in Tuscany (yes, exactly five years ago), what if I hadn't found courage to write at FIGT and then start a blog, gone to more retreats and pushed my envelope to work on a book project, now another? I am proud of it all, the words, the writings and the stories. However tough, emotional, joyous, enlightening they may or may not be. They are claimed as my own, and of our own.

The day has turned sunny, if a little breezy, and Matt reminds me of the hours that have passed. "You should take a break for yoga, Mom," he says affectionately. He sees first-hand how much better I feel, and he practices as well.

It was good to see him again after being away. He is well, but moving forward slowly. While we were away in Canada, we hoped he would make use of the money he had saved and travel. He did not, admitting he would have been too lonely. Of course, we wanted to see him take that step, and Bruce and I were initially upset and a little incredulous. I would have given anything when I was that age to have my parents live somewhere like India with its travel opportunities. But, as we know, Jo, our children are not us.

To top it off, he had not done any volunteering. Again I was angry and reminded him of the pledge he had made in Calgary five months ago. "Mom, don't let me get there and sit around," he had said through tears.

The reality was, he still needed help to 'get going' and my anger wasn't going to help. A few more afternoons were spent with him broadening his efforts yet to no avail. Finally, he reached out to an NGO contact I had given him – a school in one of Bangalore's slums that educates children with HIV and those at risk from a vast array of hardships.

Two weeks after my return, my son finally walked out of the apartment to volunteer. My relief was palpable. Seemingly a small step, but you know where we started, Jo. When he arrived back home four hours later, his words were heavy with compassion. He related some of the haunting stories, how he knew these kids deserved a chance and how drawn he was to them. He's agreed to volunteer three days a week and he'd rather make that commitment than go to Nepal

"It is important for
people to explore,
meet different kinds
of people, try jobs or
other experiences out,
fail, learn from those
mistakes and move on to
the next thing that looks
interesting, valuable and
challenging. There is
no right way or magic
passion pill."

Ellen Mahoney

where he's just been accepted by an NGO to rebuild after the earthquake. As I've related with my volunteering experience, it can have a tremendous impact on other people's lives, and what we gain is immeasurable. I hope this now for Matt.

So, hopefully, this voluntary work will be a stepping-stone to confidence as he decides upon a direction when he returns to university. It won't be until next September, but he'll start applying in the new year. For what, and where, is still undecided but I am confident that, like Andrew, things will be different the second time around. This past weekend he enrolled the three of us in a charity walk and it was great to see how he easily chatted with people we knew, as well as with strangers. He was engaged and cheerful; when he does commit to something he is 'all in'. He is moving forward.

Of course, it felt like Matt was missing this summer when we were home with the rest of the family as he had chosen to remain here. I've learned to appreciate those times, despite the fact everyone may not be under one roof. The words *resilience* and *gratitude* are the ones that come to mind when my yoga instructor asks us what our intentions are for the session. These two words are always at the forefront; they seem to be my mantra.

There is more good news as Luke will start another internship next week in the sustainability field. The three-month contract will take him and Trixie up to the period when they plan to live in Europe. After spending Christmas and a few months with us here, Luke will hopefully have secured a job in his field. Could it be the beginning of his expat journey? Will it be us visiting him one day in a far-flung location, as my parents did with us? Your phrase comes to mind… round and round it goes. But this time I say it with anticipation and with joy.

This expat life is an interesting one and I notice a book on my desk that always resonates. Linda Janssen's book title is *The Emotionally Resilient Expat… engage, adapt and thrive across cultures*. Those 10 words truly do encapsulate our life. To that sentiment I would add… *patience* and *flexibility, love* and *gratitude*, and *savour each overseas experience… enjoy the days that you can, and the ones in which you can't, well that's okay too.* Indeed, it is all part of the journey.

On that note, dear friend, I will sign off for the last time. It's been such a pleasure writing and if our words can inspire or enlighten, give comfort or even a bit of joy, then it's maybe a small gift. But then, we've already given ourselves this beautiful gift of writing. What a wonderful time it's been, Jo, I will miss this dearly. Thank you for listening and good luck with everything. I look forward to visiting; yes, The Hague, or England, is just fine!

Much love and all the best,

Terry Anne

Monday, October 2, Oslo, Norway

Dear Terry Anne,

We have decided that our six-month experiment must draw to a close. I too will miss it dearly. Thank you for the reminder of Julia Cameron and her wise words. Together with Natalie Goldberg, author of *Writing Down the Bones*, I credit them with daring me to bare my soul on the page.

And it's true, as Harry Mulisch wrote in *The Stone Bridal Bed*, the soul does 'travel by horseback'. It always takes time to recalibrate after a move or a long-haul flight. I am not surprised you need a week to settle back into a routine. In fact, I am impressed it only takes you a week.

A few days ago I was teaching my *Could Writing be Your Portable Career?* workshop and I recounted how each time we move I lose my motivation, or as I like to call it, being called Jo – my MoJo. I think it takes me a full year per posting to find my MoJo again. It is by writing letters like this that I realise we have become each other's cheerleader as we encourage and affirm each other from the sidelines. Writing letters may seem arbitrary and trite, but clearly it has tremendous value both to the writer and hopefully to the recipient.

"Each stage of your life brings different requests for your time and talent and requires adjustments to achieve the overall balance or 'ikigai' that will fit for this stage of your life."

Colleen Reichrath-Smith

This week I write from Norway, from a lovely house in the hills outside Oslo. We have spent the weekend with friends we met overseas and were invited to escape for a night to their cabin in the hills – or *hytte*. While there, without electricity, water or Wi-Fi, we watched the birds collect seeds from their feeder, foraged for chanterelles in the forest and just sat and stared or walked and looked and fed our souls from nature. It was quite wonderful. So mindful. So relaxed and, as a writer, I realised that we all need times like that in which we can simply learn to 'see' again. These letters are also teaching me to 'see' again. To see the difficulties we face and to name them and claim them.

Joshua, back from Indonesia and a stint looking after his grandpa, is now focusing on his career. He desperately needs qualifications or experience (or both) to get him started in a career as a writer on sustainability issues (funny how we each have an eco-warrior son, eh?). He is now learning to be a radio journalist, volunteering for a local expat radio station, and is blogging, also voluntarily, for the local World Wildlife Fund website. Meanwhile he is still waiting on a possible writing job in Penang and looking into journalism diplomas and internships. I am so proud of him, working 9-5 as he does on this. We have been in The Hague just over seven months and in our own house for three.

While you have seemingly circumnavigated the globe endlessly since we started writing, I have simply worn a groove driving back and forth to England. My father, it seems from the brain scan, does not have dementia, he is just old, but now he is undergoing tests for prostate cancer – so we are not out of the woods and doubt we will be. But I'm tired of constantly being on the road, preparing for a trip or recovering from one. If I am to be strong for others, or resilient, as you like to say, then I need to look after my own health. Our next trip to England, for Pa's 90th, will be by night-ferry. My next trip, in January, will be by plane and train. I can only be selfless for so long before the cracks show.

Would you believe that we have written over 50,000 words? Neither of us is in any doubt about the benefits of writing to each other regularly. Thank you for being there, for 'listening' and for being such a friend.

Bring back letter-writing, I say!

With love and all good wishes for your next move,

Jo

MONDAY MORNING EMAILS

WHAT THE EXPERTS SAY

This section offers readers the opportunity to gain a deeper understanding of topics raised within the email correspondence

 **Becky Grappo**, MEd and Certified Educational Planner, is the founder of RNG International Educational Consultants, LLC. Using her professional background as an international educator, and personal experiences as a veteran expat and mother of three adult TCKs, she works with families around the world as they navigate the challenges of educating their children and adolescents. RNG International's expert consultants work with all kinds of situations: from boarding school, therapeutic school, and programme placements all the way to university planning for students, and young adult programmes for those who are struggling with life's challenges.

To find out more, visit www.rnginternational.com

Topics covered by Becky: *Letting Go, Sibling Support, Long-distance Parenting and Staying Relevant, Contract Signing for Discipline, Emotionally Absent and Unconfident Parents, Helping Kids Make Decisions, Education Choices and TCKs, TCKs Rejecting Parents' Lifestyle Choices, Influence of House-help, Moving With Teenage Kids*

Letting go

For expat parents far away from their young adult children, it can be excruciating to know when to let kids figure things out for themselves and when to be there to offer support. No doubt, many parents feel especially guilty when they are far away in another country and can't physically be there to participate in problem-solving. That's when it's important for parents to know how to judge the severity of a situation – is it something that needs urgent, professional attention? If so, then it's important to know the who, what, when, where and how of a surrogate support team. However, if it's part of the normal bumps and bruises of emerging adulthood, then the physical distance might actually be a blessing. Not being there to rush in and problem-solve for your child also gives them the opportunity to practise some life skills that will lead to their own resiliency. That's when the parent has to let go – even if it means their child might make a mistake. Parents just need to be sure it's not the kind of mistake that has life-changing consequences.

Relying on other children to support their siblings

Many expat families have reported that sibling relationships can be especially close since the frequent moves and transitions mean siblings rely on one another to be that constant friend in their lives. Many TCKs tend to want to remain close in that special relationship, even in young adulthood, so they might be the first to notice that something is not going right in the life of their sibling. For parents who are far away, it's a relief to know that there are extra eyes and ears that can pick up on news you need to know. However, this is also an issue in which it is best to 'proceed with caution'. Depending on the situation, there might be too much responsibility and pressure on a sibling to report, monitor, negotiate and counsel their brother/ sister in crisis. It's also very important to support both children equally, and to relieve the sibling with the big shoulders of some of the psychological burden of being his/ her 'brother's keeper'.

Do parents become irrelevant if they are away too long?

Parents are never irrelevant, even expat parents. True, when parents are further away and it takes longer to get to their kids, it may seem like they are absent and have situationally 'abandoned' their child. Distance also allows young adult children to assert more independence and not become overly reliant on their parents. However, with communications in our modern world, parents and children can be more connected than ever before with the electronic umbilical cords of mobile phones, WhatsApp, Skype, Instant Messaging, texting, and the like. Furthermore, social media apps like Snapchat, Facebook, Instagram and even just sharing pictures with phones help to keep that attachment strong by sharing everyday moments together. Being able to stay in touch so easily means families can remain close and feel like they really aren't so far away after all.

Getting kids to sign a contract

Forging agreements with young adult children may not be the easiest task in the world, but clarifying expectations and the consequences of failing to live up to them might save a lot of heartache down the road. Whether the contract is about the expectation for what they will do with time off, with parentally provided funds or about behavioural goals and boundaries – and even promises around sobriety – a contract can put it all down in writing with signatories who have agreed to the contents. Many parents are reluctant to write such agreements, or young adults may chafe at consenting to them. However, depending on the circumstances it might be just the tool the family needs to develop. There are actually therapists who work with family systems and who can help the family put a home contract in place if needed.

What is an emotionally absent parent and how does this affect teenagers?

Teenagers. Many times they act as if their parents were the most annoying creatures on the planet and their presence is unwanted. But actually, most teenagers – despite the prickly outer skin of some – really do want their parents to be a part of their lives. When parents are preoccupied with their own careers, social lives or worries in the world, teenagers can feel like their parents are missing in action. Some shrug and move on; others act out to call for attention in negative ways. Often the result of an emotionally absent parent is a stronger alignment with peers, who might not be the greatest influence on the teen. Another serious consequence, though, is the child who will feel emotionally disconnected and be vulnerable to increased risk of depression and/ or anxiety.

International transitions can be particularly hard on family life, for just when children and teenagers need their parents the most for support, their parents might be totally overwhelmed with a new job, city, or country themselves. If things start to feel like they are spiralling out of control, it's important to reach out for professional counselling and mental health support.

Unconfident parents

Most parents have points in their lives as parents when they wonder what they are doing and have periods of self-doubt.

"What have we done to our children?" is a question frequently asked by many expat parents.

"What if we had done this, instead of that?"

"Was it a mistake to move to _____?"

"Maybe we should have stayed?"

"Or gone?"

"Maybe our child would have had continuity and been happier in a boarding school?"

"Oh no… maybe sending our child to boarding school was a huge mistake?"

It's important to validate that most conscientious parents do question themselves, their decisions and their life choices at some point (or maybe all the time!). But ask yourself this: did you do the best you could with what you had, or what you knew, at the time? Do your children know that you love them unconditionally? When you make a mistake, do you ask for forgiveness? When they make mistakes, do they ask for forgiveness? Perfect families only exist in fiction. Real families have conflict. They struggle. They fight. But strong families, even with imperfect parents and imperfect kids, always come back to the table to keep working on that imperfect institution we call family life.

Helping kids make decisions

Most conscientious parents want their children to grow up able to face their adulthood with confidence and purpose. But how do they get there? Big goals are met by reaching smaller goals along the way. What subjects should they study? What kind of school would serve their needs best? Where should they pursue post-secondary education? And in what country? What career path should they choose? Too much parental control over these decisions can cripple young adults' own independent decision-making later in life; too little and adolescents and young adults with relatively little life experience can get off course. It is difficult for parents to know how to be supportive without being intrusive. In some situations, children put the burden of decision-making on parents as a way of deflecting ultimate responsibility – that way, if things don't go right, they can blame you. Perhaps the best place to start is by asking your son or daughter what they are hoping to get from you as parents. Is it advice? Just a sounding board? A decision made for them? Or do they just seek your blessing? Learn to listen and ask lots of questions to help them learn how to answer them for themselves.

Should parents voice what they notice about their children's strengths?

Most parents are keen observers of their own children and know them inside and out. That includes both their strengths as well as relative areas of weakness. As children travel through adolescence and young adulthood, they are often overwhelmed with negative self-talk about all the areas in which, in their eyes, they do not excel. This is when it can be extraordinarily helpful for them to hear about their talents, skills and strengths from their parents who know them best. They are smart enough to see through false praise, yet they will probably bristle when they hear criticism. Most adolescents already have that negative track playing in their heads over and over again. Kind, loving assertions about the areas in which they excel or are strong will become their own internal dialogue over time.

Guiding children to make the right choices about education

Deciding on educational choices when children are younger falls into the area of parental responsibility. Responsible parents understand their children's learning style and needs, and hopefully will choose the right school to meet their child's needs at the post of their assignment. For some students, their needs might be best met in a boarding school, and this is also a decision-making process that should involve the student and parents. However, determining the next best steps for post-secondary becomes more complicated. For most students, this is one of the first major life decisions they will make and it is one with huge financial and life/career implications. Many international schools have strong university counsellors who can help students to discern their options; other parents might seek out the advice of a professional educational consultant who can guide their teen through the maze of higher educational options. Yet ultimately, these decisions remain important issues for the family to discuss. After all, who knows and loves this child more than the parents? And who will be financially responsible for the choices their child would like to make? These conversations will hopefully take place over time in an atmosphere of mutual respect and recognition of the needs and wants of the student as well as the family.

TCKs rejecting parents' lifestyle choices

Some TCKs grow up loving the expat lifestyle and find the multiple moves exciting and the constant change addictive. They may aspire to a globally-mobile lifestyle themselves one day. Others may have enjoyed parts of the lifestyle and be hooked on the thrill of travel and meeting those who are different from themselves, yet they do not wish to keep travelling in their own adulthoods. And still others reject the expat lifestyle completely – they long for stability and wish for a deep sense of belonging and connection somewhere. So much depends on the personality of the adolescent or young adult and their own experiences as an expat child. But parents might want to prepare for – and not be hurt – when their older children let them know in no uncertain terms that the lifestyle of constant change is not what they want for themselves. Even within the same family, children will have different reactions to moving and transitions. Some parents may feel like the rejection of the lifestyle is the same thing as the rejection of themselves and all they accomplished in their lives. To those parents, perhaps the message of 'to each his own' is the most appropriate response.

Influence of house-help

One of the perks of expat life in many countries around the world is the benefit of household help. From cooks to gardeners to maids to drivers, life is often easier in some ways overseas when there is liberation from the drudgery of daily chores. This, however, can lead to kids growing up with a false sense of reality if they hail from a country where such help is not available and, in some cases, they may even grow up with a sense of entitlement. That said, there are tens of thousands of kids who grow up with domestic help who are still appreciative of all that they have. In fact, they may even look upon those who were on the household staff as members of their own families. Those who have been caregivers and nurturers often remain in the hearts of TCKs. Therefore, one should be aware of the sense of loss and grief that may come when it is time to say goodbye to these extensions of the family. Often these losses are not recognised, so when talking to a TCK about a past assignment it might be more conducive to a deeper conversation to ask them: "What or who did you leave behind?" instead of the more vague: "What was it like there?"

Moving when kids are teens

If you ask experienced expat parents when the easiest time to move a child is, they will probably say moving younger children is easier. Parents can control activities, play dates and, to some degree, supervise the new children allowed into their children's lives. But when they get to be teenagers, it's not so easy to manage. After all, what 16-year-old wants their mum to arrange a play date? It becomes particularly tricky to move a teenager, for the teenage years are when the adolescent is individuating from the parents and finding his/ her own identity and voice. What happens if they move and all of a sudden become invisible? Who sees them? Who knows their story? Are they able to connect and find new, fulfilling, healthy relationships? Often a difficult transition can be a trigger for a mental health issue like anxiety or depression. It helps enormously when students have a portable skill or interest so that they can plug into their new school community. But adolescent years are not easy even if kids don't move, so it's critically important for parents to invest in the relationships they have with their teens. Go places. Do things together. Have family dinners. Talk. And perhaps most importantly – listen.

TCKs and changing university several times

Some of the very positive attributes of many TCKs is that they like diversity and thrive on change and new experiences. Another not-so-positive attribute is that, for the TCK who moves a lot, when the going gets rough one option can often be for them to just pick up and move due to a new assignment. Or if there is a conflict with someone else, maybe that person will move. Wheels up, problem solved. 'The problem' has magically gone away. Thus, is it so surprising that many TCKs find that when they hit a bump at university, one option for dealing with it is to transfer to a new university? Additionally, those 'bumps' might occur because of weak or non-existent interpersonal relationships, which are exacerbated by the 'TCK-otherness', or perhaps a lack of academic preparedness for university-level work in their home country. Other complications might include a learning difference, ADHD or mental health issue like depression or anxiety. Add to that the possibility of substance use on university campuses as a way of self-medicating, and one has a volatile situation. Therefore, when a young adult calls home and wants to transfer, it's advisable to dig deeper and ask more questions about what is really behind it.

Ian Moody has taught in a variety of schools for more than 35 years, including the past 15 years in international schools. He has been a school counsellor for 20 years, having obtained his Master's Degree in Educational Counselling in Nebraska, USA. He has previously taught Mathematics, Physics and English as an Additional Language and has lived in Japan, USA, Australia and Singapore. He loves working in an international context and is a strong advocate for developing good working relationships in a school community. He is a father of two TCKs (Max 25 and Georgia 19, both now living in Australia.) His wife Amanda was a trailing spouse in Singapore for a year before joining The British Council and is now a director of the Professional Development Centre. Ian is currently Head of Counselling at UWCSEA Dover, Singapore.

To contact Ian, email: imo@uwcsea.edu.sg

Topics covered by Ian: *Husband and Wife Relationship, Adult Kids Living Free at Home, Sandwich Generation and Distant Parents, Keeping Hobbies Alive For Both Women and Men, Discipline Methods, 'Breadwinner' Issues In A Mobile Family, Declining a Job Because of Family, Planning for Elder Care.*

Relationship with husband – maintaining it despite family pressures

Let us consider the notion of a relationship. It means different things to different people and includes expectations, beliefs and values, as well as the way we think about a relationship. And this is one of the challenges both men and women face in any relationship: men and women think differently. We fundamentally need to be on the 'same page' to make any relationship work. With all the pressures of family life – let alone the challenge of transition issues – we must make sure we try to, as Steven Covey, author of *The Seven Habits of Highly Effective People*, says, "Understand first and then be understood". Spend time alone with each other (date night, watch a movie, dinner, walk the dog together) but most important is the discussion that happens during this time together. If you are worried, say something. If you are happy, or pleased because they are safely back from a trip, acknowledge it. Probably one of the biggest mistakes couples can make is to assume the worst outcome possible. This may include faithfulness, risky behaviour, safety and security issues. It is a positive mindset and trust that will get you both through these doubts and insecurities. However, be courageous to say what is on your mind. Talking is very therapeutic; it is authentic and free. What more could you ask for?

Is it okay to let our adult kids live at home for free while they job hunt?

Whether to allow your adult kids to live at home is a family value issue. Do you really want to be an empty nester or are you responding to the grief associated with a child moving away from home? Both involve responding to change, and what is important is to consider the impact of how we feel, what we are thinking and how we act in these situations. Of course, we all know how difficult it is for a young person to find a job let alone worry about accommodation (including cooking, cleaning, roommates, hygiene and such). These all evoke emotional responses so try to be alert to these and freely discuss how these feelings impact on what you are thinking and your associated actions.

I think all families are torn between letting go and being there when a young adult needs you the most. It is a time-sensitive issue, when is the best time to set them free. However, make sure you both agree as to the best way forward – it is a partnership after all. Include your young adult in the discussion because it needs to be spoken about. If they live under the same roof as you then it's your right to set the expectations. Don't hope they will do the right thing, expect it! As for costs, it may be initially they cannot afford to contribute towards food costs and so on. Raise it as a discussion point, provide options and let them choose what is best for all. (Make sure ownership of the problem belongs to the young adult.) Examples of options may be to pay a small amount per week, set up an interest- free loan or do it for free. All options have consequences, however.

Sandwich generation and being torn between caring for distant parents and children

As a global nomad, I think guilt is a very strong emotion that tugs at the heartstrings all the time. It is especially evident when you see changes in your own family: siblings growing up, living in a different country to you and particularly ageing parents. Trying to balance these priorities with those of your partner can create tension in a relationship. Other issues include who gets to visit your children and/ or parents and how often and how long do they stay. The major breadwinner may be resentful if they often are left behind to work while their partner is perceived to be enjoying family time. A fair division of time visiting various family members is not only fair but can be relationship-saving. And there are special festive occasions like birthdays, anniversaries and weddings – all family events that can be challenging. I do think that going back to your roots, perhaps visiting common places of interest, honeymoon places – or even people – as well as theatre, museums, musical acts or performances from the past build a connection to what brought you and your partner together in the first place. All are good memories and guaranteed to put a smile on both of your faces.

Keeping hobbies alive – men too!

With modern technology these days, it is really important to keep up with the generation our children most identify with. Facebook, Skype, Facetime and Messenger all have a role in keeping the connection between family members current and relevant. It is authentic communication, real-time and gives you instant feedback on how the family is going. So these represent and may even constitute challenging new hobbies or activities for some of us, but with persistence and grit, looking at the positive, there can be long-term gain (with some pain perhaps). However, consider it is most likely members of our family (such as elderly parents) may have a different view of these activities and may even be fearful of them. So tread carefully.

As for keeping your old hobbies alive, the concept of walk and talk in a men's group is quite vital. We need to be doing something side-by-side to open up – a two-hour walk on a Sunday morning with a social drink at the end may seem like heaven to some but painful for others. I know of a Men's Shed concept in Australia (https://mensshed.org/) where men gather in a neighbourhood shed making things and talking at the same time. This has great benefits in helping men overcome or reduce the impact of mental health concerns. I belong to a Sunday morning walking group in Singapore where we explore the island, keep a blog of our experiences and have wonderful connective talks during the hike. So it is about being active and proactive. Use it or lose it, as they say – and this applies to past and newly acquired hobbies/ activities that mentally and physically stimulate us in an age-appropriate way.

Discipline methods

Discipline can cause major rifts in every family, especially if it is not seen by all parties as fair. Fairness is always seen in the eye of the beholder but, as mentioned previously, with clear household rules in place negotiated by all stakeholders, discipline becomes a 'firm but fair' exercise. Therefore be clear about what you expect or will tolerate. Have appropriate consequences in place: for example, a curfew. If your child comes in one hour later than expected, next time they will be coming home one hour earlier, no negotiation.

Sometimes you may have to use your intuition as to what happened. Do not look for who is to blame as we often get it wrong. Try the restorative practices (Family Group

Conference) approach when there is disagreement between siblings. Many schools are implementing this practice with considerable success in reducing behavioural concerns.

To find out more, visit: https://www.iirp.edu/what-we-do/what-is-restorative-practices/defining-restorative/22-5-3-family-group-conference-fgc-or-family-group-decision-making-fgdm

A few tips about discipline:

Make sure you and your partner agree to discipline strategies: when is it necessary, what are the consequences? Try to avoid the 'good cop, bad cop' scenario. It puts a huge strain on the relationship.

Under no circumstance should naughty children compromise your marriage. You are not their friend, you are their parent and do this together, in sync. It is a numbers game – two against one naughty child – so play the odds, and you'll win every time.

Look after your own mental health and well-being. Kids tend to exploit any opportunity when there is a perceived gain. You have to be on top of your game to address the behavioural issues, especially if there is only one parent home at the time.

Try to understand the purpose behind the behaviour. Is it attention seeking, are they hungry, bored or just tired themselves, did they have a bad night of sleep or a bad day at school? Or maybe it is just the hormones (puberty average age is about 10 years old now)?

Issues of being the breadwinner in an internationally mobile family

A number of issues to consider as the main breadwinner include being absent for various times (job requirement), keeping the family happy, especially the trailing spouse and trying to please everybody (such as where to live, what car to get, what school, being around to see the kid's activities at school, enjoying holidays together, time with your partner, financial issues like spending, pocket money for kids, helper or not and so on). Good financial planning in a shared sense is critical. Be realistic yet inclusive. Have a family discussion about the issues, and ask opinions from all stakeholders. The lifestyle sounds glamorous, but it can be stressful. Manage your emotions by taking a few seconds to pause and reflect on any decision to act – especially when it comes to finances. Ultimately, work out why you are doing this journey of discovery. Have a clear purpose, set realistic goals, monitor and review these as a family. What about the future? Do you have a long-term plan? When will you repatriate back home? Dealing with the unknowns can be a challenge. Most importantly, prepare thoroughly before the move. Read up on the many books available on transition. Set up a family book club to discuss these resources.

Declining a job because of the family

Emotionally and career-wise this can be a big decision. 'Taking a hit for the team' comes to mind as sometimes putting other family needs ahead of our own is very noble but can lead to resentment later on. Plan long term and take the view as one door closes another may open. To help you make the best decision for the family, do a SWOT analysis (https://en.wikipedia.org/wiki/SWOT_analysis) or PMI (Positives, Minuses, Interesting) that will help you work out what to do.

There are several reasons why a job offer may seem too good to be true from a family perspective. Consider the broader impact on family disruptiveness before making a commitment to a new job. Things to consider: what stage of school the kids are at, impact on immediate family from both sides, costs involved (salary, taxation, expenses, moving costs), emotional fallout (what if everyone is unhappy, resentful, will you be blamed?) as well as material things (buying new furniture, selling the family home may be considered, leaving behind the favourite places – coffee shop, restaurant, playground, holiday place and so on). From an emotional point of view, fathers may want to appear decisive so rejecting a job may seem to be weak. Develop an assertive mindset, express how you feel about the decision and let people know what you want to see happen. Carefully consider personal values, beliefs, thoughts and even myths that exist when a decision like job rejection is made. Is it really best for the family or is it more convenient? How much grit and resilience do you actually have? It becomes a personal reflection exercise – this is true, authentic learning.

Planning for elder care when you can't be around

This issue depends on your family situation as some families have siblings prepared to shoulder the load for elder care and others expect it to be fairly distributed. For me, it is about quality time rather than how often you visit or how much money you send for care. Quality time can be a visit for a week, or staying for extended periods of time and doing a range of activities that the elderly person enjoys. I have found that even when I lived in the same city and visited my elderly mother once a week for 30 minutes, this did not equate to a one-week visit every three to four months. Daily visits for a few hours each day for me built a much stronger connection. Of course, everyone is different in this view so do what you feel most comfortable doing. Discuss the options with family members and recognise the emotions at play here. Grief from leaving a loved one behind, guilt that other family members are doing more and general sadness that you are not there to see and respond to the ageing process first-hand are all tough emotions to deal with. Give yourself permission to experience these emotions that are all very real and normal.

In terms of where your elderly loved ones are located (family home, with relatives or elderly care facility) all options provoke emotional reactions amongst family members. Rarely will a family agree to what is best for an elderly parent, but research all options thoroughly as you will find your elderly parent could resist the move and create additional unexpected problems (psychological, social, emotional and physical). If a move to a care facility has been decided, spend the time visiting the facility, talking to residents' families, staff and the residents themselves. The glossy brochure is not always what you get so ask as many questions as possible to reassure all members of the family that the facility in question is going to deliver what is expected. Plan thoroughly and try to anticipate the challenges these facilities will invariably present.

Amanda Graham owns and runs a private therapeutic retreat centre in South West France. She is a Psychotherapist and yoga teacher and has recently completed her MSc in Clinical Psychology. Over the past 30 years, she has counselled families, couples, teenagers and adults. She began her working career for the UK government supporting and mentoring young people in crisis. She then went on to work with vulnerable adults with mental health issues in the community, as well as those released from prison and with problems associated with addiction. Since 2000, she has worked privately with clients in many different cultures and become a yoga teacher and Ayurvedic counsellor after studying for several years in Malaysia. She strives to deliver a combination of empirically-proven psychological treatments with a natural and holistic approach to health and well-being. At Praana Wellness, she offers a place of refuge, recovery and relaxation, and her doors are open to everyone.

To find out more, visit: www.praanawellness.com

Topics covered by Amanda: *Natural therapies, Insomnia and Sleep, Nutrition, Meditation, Yoga, Fermented foods, Health implications in difficult cities, Sourcing nutritious food.*

Natural therapies

Natural and alternative therapies are gaining prominence now in a world where we have, as societies, become dependent on a symptomatic quick-fix culture. As human beings, we are busier than ever, more stressed and anxious, and eating to survive rather than eating for our health – as a result our health services worldwide are buckling under the pressure of growing dis-ease. As an Ayurvedic practitioner, yoga teacher and counselling psychologist, I truly believe that educating people (especially young people) how to balance and treat themselves naturally through diet and alternative supplementary therapies is the way forward to living a long and healthy (and therefore happy) life. While there is always a place for general medicine in both physical and psychological disorders, it is my firm belief that this shouldn't be our first port of call. Take ownership of your symptoms; they are there to tell you something. Reach for natural therapy first. Something as simple as a yoga or meditation class, a massage, using essential oils and your very own kitchen cupboard herbs and spices, or making simple changes to your lifestyle could make such a difference to your health and well-being.

Insomnia and the importance of sleep

Without a doubt, and next to diet, good sleep is the most important element to good health and well-being. Not only the length of time you sleep, but how you prepare for sleep and the quality of your sleep are all the independent variables that measure whether you wake up feeling fresh and energised or not! Throughout our lives we become obsessed with our sleep patterns, as children and as adults. Many women particularly suffer after they have transitioned through menopause and they suffer in different ways. Why? Because we are all different body types, our bodies don't all require the exact same amount of sleep and not even at the same times. Our digestive fire 'Agni' deep drives the engine of our body and what we do with that engine dictates the strength of the fire.

While we are in sound sleep our bodies heal, cells are renewed, strengthened and even replaced through our sound and steady breathing. We must prepare for this by making sure that we quieten the mind and body before we go to bed. We must resist the temptation to stimulate the mind before we go to bed and we must resist stimulating the mind upon awakening during the night. No phones or computers – even books are thought to be stimulating. The Ayurvedic texts suggest meditation or yoga nidra before bed to aid sleep. During the night there are a series of yoga breathing exercises (known as Pranayama) you can do to aid returning to a restful slumber.

Nutrition

Think back for a moment, two generations ago, and imagine where your great-grandmother's food came from. It wouldn't have been a sandwich each day for lunch bought over a counter, it wouldn't have been a takeaway or a visit to a restaurant in the evening and it wouldn't have been in the form of vastly expensive superfoods from places in the world we can't even pronounce – let alone know where they are. How often do you have a food preparation day (or half day) for the week with your meals in mind? How often do you meal plan before doing a supermarket shop? Worse still, how many of us actually shop day-by-day calling into a supermarket on the way home from a busy day and grabbing something pre-cooked for dinner?

It's very simple. Unimaginable change has happened in these two generations. We have everything readily available to us now and many have the income to pay for it – but why should we? Well, it's a simple answer: nutrition. The absence of dis-ease and inflammation in the body begins with nothing more than good nutrition, so says Ayurveda. A good balanced diet, consisting of varied and colourful vegetables at every meal, is the simplest way to ensure your body has a head-start to health. Getting to know your own body and its individual needs helps you to plan the right nutrition for you. Being sugar-aware (there are so many hidden sugars that our bodies can't metabolise) and resisting processed foods is also a sure way to support your own health and well-being. If you are in doubt about your own nutrition, take your diet back to basics, cook from scratch and enjoy the preparation – the taste and nutrition in food lovingly prepared is a world away from that carton, packet or tin. What changes can you make to improve your nutrition?

Meditation

I was introduced to yoga and meditation after an accident in 2001. I was in much pain, frustrated and bored and unable to return to my job. I met a Buddhist monk! Yes, just like that. In a leafy affluent village on the outskirts of Bath I met a Buddhist monk walking along our country lane. I have practised since. Not always daily, sometimes twice daily, sometimes for hours and sometimes for five minutes. Sometimes when I am walking, sometimes formally sitting in the challenging Lotus pose, but my point is that meditation is available anytime, anywhere and in any situation. It is my anchor, my strength, my resilience to life's challenges; it's my simple awareness of being in the moment, and the benefits are endless.

Meditation can regulate blood pressure, increase lung function, reduce anxiety and stress, improve mood, oxygenate the bloodstream and teach self-acceptance. What is meditation? Meditation is a practise of sitting quietly and withdrawing your senses inward so you resist becoming involved in any sensory action: hearing, seeing, smelling, tasting and touching. It can be challenging for those who find it difficult to stand still, people with high energy. Some people who like control will tell you they simply can't meditate. Truth is: anyone can meditate, but it's a practise and one must allow the time for this practise if one is to receive the benefits.

Yoga

I teach yoga four times a week to groups, both adults and children. I teach yoga on a one-to-one basis to people who have limitations physically and I use certain yoga techniques to aid clients when they are in therapy. Yoga has a plethora of benefits for all. It has also, in the West, become an exceptionally lucrative business and quality has, in my opinion, in some cases, been compromised.

There are eight limbs to Patanjali's Hatha yoga and the physical aspect that we are so familiar with is only one of those elements. Yoga, if practised in the true sense, is a philosophy of life; it affects every aspect of our lives, how we think, how we act, how we treat people and, first and foremost, how we treat ourselves. Right diet, balance in everything and possibly a spiritual connection are all tied up with yogic lifestyle. It is important to find a style of teaching that is right for you and a teacher you can connect with. It is important to ask yourself what it is you need from a yoga practice: is it relaxation, energy, strength or all of these? Then find the class that will offer you what you need.

Fermented foods

It is estimated that 100 trillion microorganisms make their home in our gut, and while we are still not entirely sure of their role in our health we do know they have a role and researchers think it is big! When we eat a diet rich in fermented foods we are "lining our gastrointestinal tract with healthy food-related organisms", says Dr Robert Hutkins, Professor at University of Nebraska-Lincoln.

I was first introduced to fermented foods at the age of 23, living in the bush in the southern highlands of Tanzania. Our German neighbours always served us sauerkraut. I ate it politely, but not understanding why. However, hindsight is wonderful. Looking back, they were super fit people in their early sixties and they ate a balanced and mostly wholefood diet and it always included a daily portion of sauerkraut!

Ayurveda says that if we do not evacuate our bowels twice a day then we are storing 'Ama' (a Sanskrit word for toxins) and this will bleed into our bloodstream and lead to dis-ease in our bodies. Dis-ease manifests in ways that present in such familiar symptoms that we often put down to ageing. So we must do what we can to prevent this happening, and to keep our gut flora healthy and active to strengthen our immune system. Fermented foods are a way of helping us to do this. Living in France now, *choucroute* proudly stands on the deli counter in the supermarket, and once again I'm reminded of the importance of fermented foods in our diet. The secret to introducing something new is to keep it simple, affordable and local – there must be a cabbage near you somewhere! Try it. Like any new healthy change, try a little and introduce it slowly. The benefits may take a week to notice.

Living in difficult cities and health implications

Do you suffer with eczema, asthma or other allergies? Do you find it challenging living in a city where there may be traffic or noise pollution or possibly industry close by? The secret to 'surviving' any environment that you may not choose to be in is to look to yourself and your own self-protection, to do what you can to stay strong and feed body and mind with positivity and happiness. My tips would be:

Try and drive out of the city every weekend – somewhere where the air is cleaner, the environment greener and be in the great outdoors.

Find a store that sells organic fruit and vegetables. If you are in doubt, steep your wholefoods in a little salted water for 10 minutes to remove any chemicals from the skins. Where you can, buy local.

Find a group of like-minded people with like-minded interests.

Use a water diffuser for purifying the air in your home with 100% natural essential oils. They make an enormous difference to the quality of the air you breathe. They also relieve many common irritants and ailments associated with city living.

Use good supplements to help strengthen and support where perhaps our diet is lacking.

Find a yoga practice if you struggle to stay positive about your surroundings. Yoga is known to aid physical and mental well-being in the most difficult of circumstances and surroundings.

Finally, we all have choices. Sometimes they are difficult, risky, unknown. If you know your environment really is making you ill then you must consider a change.

Sourcing nutritious food

It's quite simple: if you value your physical and mental health you must source nutritious food. Nutritious food is our 'medicine', fast and processed food or food full of refined sugars is our 'poison'. I grew up in a city where most of our neighbours grew some lettuce and tomatoes in their front gardens in the summer months. (When I ventured down this road a year or so ago most of the gardens were now concrete and accommodating two or three cars!). Here in rural France, all of my neighbours have very impressive and very simple rows of all-year-round vegetables. They preserve what they can't eat. Of course, they have more space… but even that is not really a valid excuse now. So what has changed? Is it our priorities? Are we just time short and far too busy (and are we busy with stuff that takes precedence over health?) or do we simply accept dis-ease is more recurrent as we age?

I have lived in countries where we could only live on what we grew and doctors were a long way away. I have lived in wealthy countries with the sickest of people and where doctors were always busy and the drug companies happy. Taking time to prepare and source nutritious food is vital to maintaining health. We have farm shops, online vegetable deliveries and a plethora of local markets and supermarkets available to us in most countries now. Most of us have space outside with natural light to have some potted herbs, tomatoes and now we even have vertical gardens for the apartment dwellers amongst us. The most important point being we need to make time to invest in our health and that means sourcing nutritious food.

Lesley Lewis is a skilled psychologist offering counselling and coaching services. She has an MS in Education and Cross-Cultural Studies, an MS in Educational Psychology – with an emphasis in mental health – and over 35 years of experience as an educator, private therapist and trainer/ consultant working in Asia, Europe and North America. Lesley takes a warm, humanistic approach to counselling and she has developed methods for success that are specifically designed for expatriates and/ or in cross-cultural environments. In her coaching, she works with sojourners, expats and locals to produce desirable and effective results that are not only applicable to business, but also to personal life-balance. She also provides cross-cultural training to relocated employees from some of the largest financial and investment multinationals in the world.

To find out more, visit: http://www.laurenbramleymd.com and/ or http://culture3counsel.com/

Topics covered by Lesley: *When your kid mentions suicide, what to do? The case for and against medication, Genetics and family heritage, The value of writing through your pain, Letter writing, How to be a good listener, Living in constant limbo, A couple putting their relationship first, Keeping joint hobbies alive, Finding time to play! When friends become family.*

When your kid mentions suicide, what to do?

If your child mentions suicide, take it seriously. So many parents think that mentioning the word is just an attention-seeking device. There are many ways to receive attention, but the word suicide is not one. Take it seriously. Keep communication open with your child as much as possible and assess the seriousness of the situation. Please, do not be judgmental with your child and what they are saying to you; listen, listen and give love. A suicidal person is feeling helpless, hopeless, and in need of the comfort of people who care for them the most.

Each situation is different, but certainly seek professional advice and assess the suicidal ideation or attempts. In many cases, counselling alone can reach the core of the issues that have led to the present situation. This will usually take the form of individual therapy, but family therapy can also be useful in some cases – again, try not to judge, but consider the child's recovery. Also, please check if there is any drug/alcohol dependency. If the situation is highly volatile, you may need to take your child to an emergency room for immediate help. Hopefully this is not necessary, but it can happen.

The case for and against medication

This is my own personal philosophy drawn from several decades' experience as a therapist. Ideally, and prior to medication being administered in the initial stages of counselling, I will ask the client to have a complete physical and a blood test and read the results. I want to make sure the person is physically healthy or if there are certain areas that might be causing them difficulty psychologically.

The second step is to ask about eating and sleeping habits and the type of exercise a person is doing. I also want to know the psychological history of the individual and his/ her family members. My approach is to try many different means, whether it be acupuncture, vitamins, minerals, diet, meditation and other treatments before I would refer someone to a psychiatrist to conduct an assessment and prescribe medication. There are some circumstances that need immediate attention – dependent on diagnosis, severity and prevailing circumstances – but generally I would refrain from instant medication.

Genetics and family heritage

Genetics often play a huge role in an individual. It is important, if possible, to know the make-up of past generations. This can give a person some indicator as to their physical, mental and emotional predispositions. If a grandparent has had strokes, heart issues or diabetes, it is important to take note of this and to share the information with a doctor when relevant. Keeping track of one's physical condition and reading up on the possible physical manifestations is also useful.

In regard to emotional and mental upsets, it has been proven in research that many conditions – for example, depression, anxiety, schizophrenia and more – often have a genetic link. It is important for parents to inform their children as they get older of the so-called 'family heritage' and what could be inherited. Another condition that has been genetically linked is alcoholism and drug-dependency. In the past, we've often heard jokes made that Grandpa 'sipped' five beers a night. This area may be more difficult to determine from past generations, as it wasn't as talked about and understood. Now, though, there are definite links one should be aware of.

If a person has an opportunity to speak to their family regarding their genetic make-up, do so. Too many families feel uncomfortable with talking about mental illness and/ or alcoholism, but it is healthy to be open about this. It is too often treated as a shameful situation, rather than making it the reality of the family. Be open, gain knowledge and be forever understanding.

The value of writing through your pain

Writing can be very cathartic. It allows an individual to express the pain they are holding inside. Writing is a release, and the privacy of your own journaling is safe. You can say anything you want and not worry or be fearful that someone else will find out about your feelings. A person can say what they want and use whatever words they want – even repeat the same thing over and over – as a way of dealing with emotions. It allows the pain to flow out, and there is no right or wrong to the writing process; one can sometimes just chronicle events, to gain understanding of a situation that has caused pain. Neither is there a right time or wrong time to write/ journal.

I always suggest that clients find an appealing notebook and cherish their journals. Some people say: "I don't know what to write." Just start with anything, it can even be about the weather. When someone is committed to their writing and journaling process it becomes part of their daily ritual, and eventually they may look forward to the process of unleashing their pain and/ or other issues. The outlet of writing is like releasing the pressure in a pressure cooker. This can help someone to feel calm by understanding the feelings that they have, and hopefully finding solace.

Narrative Therapy can be useful in allowing people to understand themselves, their values and the skills needed to live their values on a daily basis. It follows the steps of: identifying and 'telling stories' about themselves – who they are – to have a better understanding of what they want to keep and what they would like to change about themselves. The outcome is the 're-authoring' of one's identity. The client will narrate their lives and then the therapist will help to restructure a new narrative that seems to be more effective. In Narrative Therapy, we are looking at the 'True Self': one's identity. The process is done by questions and conversations, and can involve reference to the client's journal for greater insight.

Letter writing

If letters are to be received by another individual, letter writing can be an opening-up process, which gives the writer the confidence to state how they are feeling. This process requires much trust in the receiver to enable the writer to share their words. It can be very comforting to be able to share such thoughts and feelings, and thereby find release. Hopefully there is total openness for the receiver to write about the sent letter, and there can be a flow of communication. Rules may be needed at the beginning so that misunderstandings do not arise.

From reading the exchange between Jo and Terry Anne, letter writing can be so beneficial in the sharing of ideas, thoughts, feelings, experiences and a whole host of other topics in one's life. The beauty is the trust that has been created between the writers. Trust is not easy to create between people, it requires time, and the fact this has happened is beautiful.

There are times when letters are written and never sent or written. I have had clients over the years write to someone who has passed away, in order to express all the feelings that were not stated when the person in question was alive – or there wasn't the opportunity to do so due to age or the fear of self-expression. This exercise can greatly assist someone in the grieving process. At other times, it can be helpful to write to someone who *is* alive just to express how one feels. The letter does not have to be sent, but the process of writing and releasing emotions is very helpful in the therapeutic process.

How to be a good listener

Listening is one of the hardest skills that a person can learn. As children, we were always interrupted by adults, or other children, whether at school, home, gatherings and so on. As adults, most people still freely interject during conversations. Are we truly listening to what the other person is saying? Or are we just going through the motions, but in our minds thinking, *Oh, I have to go to the store and pick up coffee,* or, *I have to make a telephone call,* when someone is talking to us?

'Active listening' is when we are truly listening, no interruptions; we are totally focused on the other person. Once he/ she has spoken, we as the listener feed back into what the person has said and the dialogue continues. Too often people interrupt with their own thoughts and ideas. If this is what the person asked for in the dialogue then fine, but often people want someone just to listen without input, judgement, or saying, "Well, this is what I would have done." Engage in a dialogue; listen, listen and listen truly to what the other is saying. It is not easy.

Living in constant limbo

I feel that, as expats, we do live in a constant state of limbo. Where will the next move be? Do we stay in the Expat Life cycle forever? When is the next holiday? When's the flight 'home' to visit old friends and family? When do we make decisions to retire? Where? The questions go on and on, keeping us in a distinctly modern form of limbo. There is an aspect of the personality in most expats that thrives on the 'constant limbo'. We learn to go with the flow. Limboland. We learn to adjust better than most in this state.

Of course, there may be times when we resent this limbo: *Why can't we just settle down and have the routine like others?*

There's not always a straightforward answer. So, learning to be in the state of limbo, adjusting ourselves to live in the 'grey' area, is a healthy step forwards. Most expats, especially the 'seasoned' expats, know exactly what needs to be done to settle in quickly and get on with their lives – both professionally and personally. Getting the routine going, knowing the basics, is key to make us feel content. This limboland becomes questionable when there are difficulties that arise in our lives, and increasingly difficult to justify.

If 'limbo' is adding too much stress, too many concerns and questions, then it is time to evaluate the present moment and whether one wants to continue this lifestyle. Otherwise, learning to adapt will give you some unique and useful skills. Think about what your most pressing concerns are, and find the best solution for your circumstances.

A couple putting their relationship first

Yes, yes, and yes! When working with a couple, I will always say, "If you put your relationship first, then the rest of the family will be okay." Frequently what happens is that the children are put first, and stay in that ranking until the last one leaves home. Then, all too often, the husband and wife look at one another and realise they have grown apart, have no common interests and divorce.

Ideally, the couple will grow together over the years. Respect and communication for each other is a must, plus the trust – the basis for any relationship. Yes, work, raising children, moving to a new locale, and getting set up can interfere and

255

take priority. When this happens, the couple can wind up going out for dinner and then have little to communicate, except: "How was your day? How was work? How are the children?"; end of conversation. Keep the relationship alive with date nights, get-aways, common interests, sex, talking about everything and anything – and don't fall into a rut.

Finances, Sex and Communication are the three most common issues couples have; recognise these topics and make them healthy in your partnership. Of course, there will be rough patches along the way, there will be disagreements, and more. Learn how to resolve conflict in a healthy manner instead of silence and/ or arguing. Be gentle, loving and true to yourself in your marital relationship. I know there will be circumstances where children will need to come first, but if the partnership is strong and the two people involved know how to work together, it will strengthen their bond. Laugh often. Humour is the best.

Keeping joint hobbies alive

Hobbies are a key ingredient to our own individuality, and to us as a couple. Know what your hobbies are and pursue them, or at least pursue a few. Share hobbies with your partner, so that you can maintain similar interests. It keeps your relationship alive. So many people use the excuse (and I say excuse!): "I don't have time to pursue any hobbies." I question this statement with my clients and others in my life: "Why are you not making time?" I often hear many themes such as: "I have too much work"; "I feel guilty if I take time to do a hobby"; "I don't know what I would even do"; and so on.

There are many reasons why people don't take up hobbies, and thereby forfeit sharing a commonality with their partner. Step back and re-assess your thought process. Hobbies make you, and your relationship, come alive and stay interesting

Finding time to play!

As adults, it is imperative to find time to 'play'. Play doesn't stop at childhood. It should be a constant throughout life. If your TCKs/ ATCKs are questioning why you are playing (yikes) I would probably say to them: "Well, why aren't *you* playing?" Parents need to find time to play – throw your hands up in the air, swirl around, dance, have a good laugh – and show your children you are still laughing and playing no matter what age you are. A lack of play can petrify the atmosphere of a household, and lead to people keeping themselves to themselves.

We can be a great role model for our children. It's not taxing to be silly, to joke around, to fill in a colouring book – whatever it is. As I say to my grandson who is three years old: "Let's be goofy!" My adult children can see me playing, and they in turn start to play around.

When friends become family

As expats, we are the rare breed of people that pack up and move far from our nuclei and extended family members. Even though the numbers are growing more and more within the expat community, we are still a very small percentage. And so, yes, our friends can become like family. The annual visit, or bi-annual visit, with our family 'back home' is not the same as living with our friends through the day-to-day.

Our friends overseas go through all the same ups and downs, illnesses of children, school selections, family picnics, holidays, weekends away, partying and more. We share so much with our friends. They understand who we are, what our moods may be, and truly what is going on in our lives moment-by-moment. Our family members know from the daily or weekly Skype call, or the occasional visit, but how much they understand our lives overseas depends on the communication and how much time is spent together.

Despite moving, we often stay in contact with our global 'family' for the rest of our lives. They are our lifelines – we have lived through so much together, and they better understand the expat life and what it entails compared to a monocultural family and monocultural friends. I feel very strongly about such friendships, and how close they become.

Colleen Reichrath-Smith believes that knowing how to navigate career transitions is a vital life skill for today. That's why she teaches people to navigate their own careers across occupational boundaries, international borders and changing times, in order to create a personally meaningful portable career. In 1998 Colleen started CJS Career Consulting in Canada, and in 2006 she took her career on an international adventure to the Netherlands. In 2007, by using what she teaches, she was delivering career training again, this time in Dutch. Colleen is co-author of *A Career in Your Suitcase,* 4th Ed., and is certified as a Global Career Development Facilitator (GCDF).

To find out more, visit: www.careerinyoursuitcase.com

Topics covered by Colleen: *Being fulfilled as an empty nester, Changing habits, Retaining a global career, Trailing and identity, Re: Kristin Duncombe's issues of trailing and existential crisis, Volunteering.*

Being fulfilled as an empty nester

Each stage of your life brings different requests for your time and talent and requires adjustments to achieve the overall balance that will fit this stage of your life. It is normal as each stage presents itself that you will question and evaluate your current situation in order to see where you want to make changes, whilst continuing to achieve growth and fulfilment in this new stage.

Three models for perspective

It could be that you will need to focus energy on addressing shifts in some of the lower levels of Maslow's Hierarchy (see p. 50) before you can focus again on fulfillment. That is also part of the transition.

Using the *ikigai* model for finding meaning in your life may help you identify where you want to make adjustments to find and regain focus, balance and meaning for this new stage of life. Which feeling in the graphic below do you identify with most? Start there.

Infinity Career Development model, as described in *A Career in Your Suitcase*, p. 341. Each choice you've made at *3. Set my direction* brings new experiences, which develop new awareness for *1. Who am I?* which then brings different interactions with the world and creates opportunity to *2. Explore options* – which then leads to making a next choice. This cycle continues over the course of your life and there is no 'wrong' choice; there is only learning. Note: These steps do not always happen in this sequence.

The following publications may also be of interest: *The Physics of Living*, Norm Amundson, Ergon Communications, 2003, and *A Career in Your Suitcase*, 4th ed. Jo Parfitt, Colleen Reichrath-Smith, 2013. Start on p. 41.

Changing habits

So much can be said here. Knowing that change is constant means you can't put your life on autopilot. You will need to actively choose each day to do what you intend to do. Having a personal vision will help you keep focused and on course towards that vision. It is a tool to help you look beyond the daily routine and see the big picture.

Remember that, as Dave Redekopp states, *"Every decision – even one like choosing to get up on time in the morning – is a career decision."*

Be aware of what is motivating you on the inside and use that motivation to move forwards. Create a vision board, a desire map or a mission statement to help you keep on track. And give yourself a day off too! Danielle Laporte, in *The Desire Map* quotes: *"The journey has to feel the way you want the destination to feel."*

The following publications may also be of interest: <u>*Untethered Soul – Journey Beyond Yourself*</u>, Michael A. Singer (see the <u>Oprah Winfrey</u> interview regarding how he sees fear) and *<u>The Mobile Life</u>*, Diane Lemieux and Anne Parker (how to plan and build the life you want anywhere in the world).

Retaining a global career

Your identity grows and develops with you. In that sense it will shift as you take on different roles (life partner, parent, leader, volunteer, world traveller, global nomad) and grow in depth through the experiences each role brings. In order to stay connected with this development I suggest creating a personal archive, or *portfolio*, where you keep 'artefacts' from your life journey. These include educational achievements and your CV, as well as stories from your life – especially since there will be no 'personnel department' keeping this file for you. The stories I refer to can include pictures as well as a description of:

1. The situation

2. What needed to be done

3. What you yourself did

4. The results that were generated

5. A personal reflection on what you learned through this experience

The stories can come from every part of your life, including hobbies, volunteering, work and vacations. These stories provide connectors to 'early identities' and can support you and your identity growth through new experiences towards 'evolving identities'. A portfolio is also a great tool for your kids to see what they love to do, a way to support your children to discover their strengths and, based on these insights, make choices for their future.

To understand and gain the most insights from your experiences, the model below is useful. It starts at the top where you have an experience that stretches you: a Boundary Experience. From there you move towards your first response to it: your First Story. From there it is important to move through the four phases of Sensing, Sifting, Focusing and Understanding in order to arrive at a Second Story. During this four-phase process, you engage in internal and external dialogue that provide the transformational space in which you change and grow through the experience. It is even possible to step back from the experience into an 'observer' role to gain additional perspective on the Boundary Experience.

Source: *Career Writing*, Reinekke Lengelle, available at http://writingtheself.ca

The following publication by Jo Parfitt and Colleen Reichrath-Smith may also be of interest: *A Career in Your Suitcase*, 4th ed. I suggest you use the Portfolio Worksheet on p. 248.

Trailing and identity

When the part of you connected to your work and career becomes disassociated with the rest of your life, through embarking on an international or expat adventure, you can feel lost and unsure of who you are. You are no longer sure what to tell people when they ask, "What do you do?" I suggest thinking of career in this holistic way:

Thinking this way allows you to find a way to describe your career in a way that encompasses more of your life roles and what's important to you. To connect the lines of your identity even more strongly with your present situation, explore what has influenced your career decisions in previous contexts and at this moment. Career decisions are always made in a context and, for accompanying partners, the more you understand the influences of your shifting contexts the more you can consciously use these or choose to bring in new ones.

A Career in Your Suitcase, 4th ed. has exercises, as Jo refers to, exploring how previous generations of your family's passions, values, skills and strengths have influenced you (see p. 59). On p. 57 we ask you to explore some of your Defining Moments and use these insights to strengthen your sense of self and increase your resilience as you continue to go through life changes.

The Decision-Making Grid shared on pages 170 and 369 of *A Career in Your Suitcase* is a tool that can support you to make decisions coherent with your values, lifestyle factors and vision for your future. The grid gives these components a more objective form while still allowing room for your intuition. Within the same publication, you can also refer to the Infinity Career Development Model in Part I and the Portfolio in Part XI.

Kristin Duncombe's issues of trailing and existential crisis

Your career, in the holistic sense, is filled with transitions and change. The reality is that transitions will keep coming. Know that each time this happens, there is a cycle to work through. This can give you structure and a way to ride the wave of change instead of sinking into an existential crisis.

Develop a purpose or mission statement that is broader than your current situation. Remember the holistic definition of career (*A Career in Your Suitcase*, 4th ed, Part VII) and then explore your current reality to discover small ways you can live your mission now. Each small step or decision adds up in the big picture and the long run. Keep identifying and taking small steps towards living your mission. Remember the quote shared in Part IV: *every decision is a career decision*. You may also find the publication *Change and Transition,* by William Bridges, helpful for the transition cycle analysis work.

Volunteering

When you choose to see career from a holistic perspective, as part of your *ikigai*, then many more possibilities appear to find fulfilment. Volunteering is a valuable way to use and develop your skills to achieve results that are personally meaningful to you. Skills are transferable from one context and setting to another. When you know what skills you want to keep developing and those you want to grow, you can make choices that will support this development. These skills, your willingness to keep growing them, your awareness of them and your ability to communicate and share them, are your tickets to future possibilities.

Ellen Mahoney, MEd, is an international school alumna and TCK. She has been a teacher, counsellor and director at iMentor, a leading youth mentoring organisation in the United States recognised by President Obama and Mark Zuckerberg for its excellence and innovation. She is certified in mentoring programme supervision by Fordham University's Graduate School of Social Work. She has served on the international boards of Families in Global Transitions, I Am A Triangle and Safe Passage Across Networks. She is currently the CEO of Sea Change Mentoring, which delivers transitions-informed consulting services, programme audits, and social-emotional learning curriculum to international schools. It also provides mentoring experiences for third culture teens and emerging adults.

To find out more, visit: www.seachangementoring.com

Topics covered by Ellen: *Emerging adulthood, Challenges for ATCKs, Mental health and the emerging adult, Effective communication with our ATCKs, Parent as mentor/ counselor, Effective communication in an overseas family, Helping our young adults 'see' what they love to do.*

Emerging adulthood

When trying to figure out how to best support your ATCK, it is important to take a step back and assess what is typical for anyone at this stage in life and what is specific to ATCKs. Jeffrey Jensen Arnett coined the phrase 'emerging adulthood' to describe this time in people's lives between adolescence and "the time they enter stable adult roles in love and work". In other words, it is typically the stage between ages 18 and 29. Whereas prior generations went from adolescence directly into adult roles, like spouse and parent, Arnett observed that, particularly in middle to upper class communities in developed nations, people in their late teens and twenties were experiencing a stage that wasn't quite adolescence and wasn't quite adulthood.

Why? Because more emerging adults are postponing marriage and creating their own families until their 30s, if at all. More emerging adults are going directly to post-graduate programmes, after graduating from university, in order to find jobs in this sophisticated information and technology economy. This means that middle to upper class parents are choosing to financially support them for longer. The fortunate among the Millennial Generation and Generation Z look for careers that they will feel passionately about, that make a difference, or that will make them feel great – instead of just securing a job to pay the bills. If this means that they will not earn enough to support themselves yet, or that they have to wait months or even years to find that dream job, they are willing to wait and many parents are willing to financially support them in the meantime.

Challenges for ATCKs

You may see some of these attributes of emerging adulthood that Arnett identified in your own ATCKs:

- Identity exploration

- Instability in love, work, and residence

- Self-focus (with a very low obligation to others)

- Feeling in-between, in constant transition

- Optimism; unparalleled opportunity for life transformation

How does this differ between most of the emerging adults in this age group? The differences are few, but the intensity may be stronger. The main difference for ATCKs is that the impact of mobility, interrupted friendships and educations, unresolved grief, and other common experiences of a TCK childhood compound some of the challenges during emerging adulthood.

ATCK parents may continue to move after their children turn 18, leaving ATCKs feeling like they have no 'home base' during a time of instability. Many TCKs are told by parents as they grow up that 'the world is their oyster'; when it is time to choose how they want to make this idea come to fruition, they may simultaneously feel optimistic but also great anxiety when faced with so much choice. In addition, some parents feel guilty for having frequently moved the family, and they feel they have enabled indecision and dependence by financially supporting their emerging adolescents in an effort to repair mistakes made by their own parents.

The developmental job of an emerging adult is to learn how to make independent decisions, become financially independent, and either accept responsibility for oneself or to learn to care for parents (depending on regional cultural norms and values). Your job as a parent during this stage is to make enough space for them to learn these skills and to make efforts not to impede this progress.

Mental health and the emerging adult

While creating space for your kids to learn to be adults is important, there are times when a family has to step in quickly: when there is a serious mental health concern, and/ or when your child says directly or indirectly that they want to kill themselves or hurt someone else. In this case, when Joshua explained what was going on with him and his concerns about an LSD-triggered emotional breakdown, or in the case of Matt having the courage to tell his mother that he didn't think he could "go on", both sets of parents jumped right into action and that is positively appropriate to take such moments seriously.

A good rule of thumb comes from the psychology and education professions: if you find out that they want to kill themselves, hurt someone else or that someone is hurting them, intervene immediately. Look for any sudden change in behaviour. For example, if they typically have a lot of energy and spend time with their friends outdoors and suddenly they are sleeping most of the day and never leave the home, you have cause for concern.

If your child opens up to you, take a deep breath and focus on actively listening and acknowledging their feelings without acting on an urge to have a response ready. Remember that their experience living internationally is different than your experience. Never belittle, ignore or openly doubt their feelings. Gently but persistently encourage them to connect with their peers and family, to volunteer and get outside, and to access professional help. If they do seek out professional help, encourage them to bring along Lois Bushong's *Belonging Everywhere and Nowhere: Insights into Counseling the Globally Mobile.* You can't assume that counsellors and psychologists understand the nuances of growing up as a TCK and this book is a great reference for them.

If your child is far away, try to agree to create a regular schedule to meet via video conferencing. Facetime is important, even if that 'face-time' is through the screen of a computer. However, be open to other forms of communication as well. Sometimes it is less stifling or overwhelming to communicate in short bursts over texting apps. Other times, in order to convey what one really feels, a longer email is easier than an in-person conversation. Some young people, especially boys, prefer to avoid extended eye contact while they are talking about topics that make them feel vulnerable. Others prefer to be doing something with their hands, so consider having these conversations while cooking a meal together or cleaning out a storage space or going on a long drive. Alternatively, as we see here with Joshua, particularly, they may ask you for your total attention. Take their cues and turn off your cell phone. In other words, meet them where they are when it comes to the kind of technology and environment they may need to open up.

When offering to support your child, try to give them a choice in the kind of help they may require. You can say something like, "We can offer you two kinds of support: you can come live with us as long as you see a psychologist and find a part-time job, or we can pay for you to see a psychologist on your own and we must have a family Skype meeting every Sunday for the next three months to check in." As privileged as so many TCKs can be, choosing where we are going and who we will say goodbye to has rarely been an option. It is a wonderful change of pattern to share that kind of power with emerging ATCKs.

Finally, familiarise yourself with the warning signs of a person contemplating suicide. A great resource on this topic and all other mental health concerns is Australia's Headspace (www.headspace.org.au)

Effective communication with our ATCKs

The experience of Matt visiting India and commenting on the poverty they witness is such a Third Culture Family moment, and an opportunity for meaningful reflection. Just like feelings of loss, powerlessness, or rootlessness that many TCKs experience, our feelings about wealth disparity are equally important to express to one another and grapple with together as a family.

How do we develop the vocabulary to address our feelings, whatever they may be? If you can, get a head start when your children are young. Build an emotional vocabulary together, practise telling the stories of what you are experiencing throughout this international existence, and be aware of your own emotional responses and what you are modelling for your children. In her book *Emotional Resilience and the*

Expat Child: Practical Tips and Storytelling Techniques that will Strengthen the Global Family, Julia Simens explains, "the ability to name a feeling will allow your child to discuss and reflect with you about his or her personal experience of the world. The larger your child's vocabulary, the finer discrimination he or she can make between each of their separate feelings and the better they can communicate with others about these feelings." Her book is a great resource with activities and advice for families getting a head start.

If you feel that you weren't able to do this with your children when they were younger, please know that it is never too late. Parenting, as we all know, does not come with an instruction manual and no one ever gets it perfectly right. The good news is we understand more and more how to fix conflicts in families and how to repair communication breakdowns. For more on this topic, I think every parent should read Daniel Siegel and Mary Hartsell's book *Parenting From the Inside Out: How A Deeper Self-Understanding Can Help You Raise Children Who Thrive.*

Parent as mentor/ counsellor – does it work?

The listening techniques that Jo talks about here can be so helpful in communicating with your children. In fact, these are similar techniques that we suggest our mentors use at Sea Change Mentoring. While parents can be great advisors, listeners, and encouragers, traditional mentors can play a very special role in the life of an ATCK. According to youth mentoring researcher Jean Rhodes, mentoring describes a "relationship between an older, more experienced adult and an unrelated, younger protégée. The mentor typically provides ongoing guidance, instruction, and encouragement aimed at developing the competence and character of the mentee."

It is developmentally appropriate for adolescents and emerging adults to move from getting most of their emotional needs met by their parents to getting most of these needs met by a diversity of peers, mentors, teachers and romantic partners. One aspect of such relationships is this sense of belonging. As Sam mentions, his peers "get him". This is a mirroring that happens in adolescent and emerging adult friendships that is quite important and helps young people feel connected and legitimate or accepted. It can be quite a powerful thing for ATCKs to find mentors that not only can provide guidance and encouragement but who can also mirror their identities as ATCKs. This is why all of our mentors at Sea Change Mentoring are also ATCKs. You can learn more at www.seachangementoring.com or read about the power of mentoring at MENTOR (www.mentoring.org).

Effective communication within the family

With families living around the world, either together or apart, sometimes we have to get creative in finding ways to communicate. Take advantage of the technology that is out there. Start a private family Pinterest, Facebook, or Instagram account and drop in pictures from your daily lives wherever you are and images or videos that pique your interest. Create a family WhatsApp group or Slack community and stay in touch, write stories, tell jokes or share favorite recipes. Creating family rituals, traditions and spaces are a great way to foster a deeper connection between each other and a shared memory of the past. Technology can help your family document, reflect, and celebrate together.

Helping our kids 'see' what they love to do

I avoid the word 'passion' when helping young people figure out what next step to take in their lives. Only a minority of people can say they found that one thing they were passionate about and everything after that fell into place. In fact, in the book *Designing Your Life: How to Build a Well-Lived, Joyful Life* by Bill Burnett and Dave Evans, the authors observe that 80% of people they have researched don't have any idea what they are passionate about. They write that William Danton, of the Stanford Center on Adolescence, found that one in five people between the ages of 12 and 25 know "where they want to go, what they want to accomplish in life, and why."

We use the word passion so often that some young people become filled with anxiety because they haven't found their passion yet as if 'finding your passion' sets everything right and the path becomes crystal clear. Life and personal success simply doesn't work that way. Instead, it is more important for people to explore, meet different kinds of people, try jobs or other experiences out, fail, learn from those mistakes and move on to the next thing that looks interesting, valuable and challenging. There is no right way or magic passion pill. Still, there are ways to make the overwhelming task of figuring out what to do next with one's life a little easier. I highly recommend that ATCKs read the aforementioned book by Evans and Burnett in order to create a plan to a create a life, career and family that will make them happy and which will create value for others.

Nell Smith is the author of the industry-respected, motivational *Retire to the Life You Love, Practical Tools for Designing Your Meaningful Future,* a self-help guide for men and women that is packed with ideas, tools, examples and stories to help you plan your own fulfilling next chapter of your life in the new age of longevity. Now in her own third age, Nell's background as a professional in the fields of career development, adult education and conscious ageing has led to her 20 plus years working as a Registered Retirement Consultant.

To find out more, visit: www.retiretothelifeyoulove.com

Topics covered by Nell: *Is retirement the end of your life? When and how to start retirement planning, The stages of retirement.*

Is retirement the end of your life?

In broad terms, retirement is a social construct that no longer fits our current longevity. Consider that at 65, the traditional retirement age, we can expect to live on average another 20 years. Some of us will live much longer, to even 100 or more, but let's work with the number 20. Twenty years is another lifetime and a whole new career where anything is possible. Many of us will remain fit, healthy and actively engaged in life with vitality and zest for the whole 20 years and beyond.

This next stage is therefore not the end of our life adventures, but a new beginning full of potential, possibilities and opportunities. Life continues as a metaphorical journey, not a single destination, and with a whole new chapter and blank pages ready for you to decide how you will continue your personal story.

Tips for how to know when to move on to your next life chapter:

1. When the pull for something different is stronger than the pull of the old.

2. When you have ideas of what you'd like to retire *to*, rather than dwelling on what you're retiring *from*.

3. When your level of potential future income supports your choices and interests.

Considerations and questions to ask yourself:

1. Move where you want to put down roots, not necessarily where your adult children and your grandchildren reside as they may move instead of you, leaving you behind.

2. Determine the importance of climate and scenery for each of you. If your preferred location does not have the climate/ scenery you enjoy, consider holidaying there instead.

3. Consider the need for health care services now and in the future. How close do you want to be to those services? What if you can no longer drive yourself?

4. Choose between an urban or rural location. Consider what it is that appeals in each. Can you get the best of both in one location, such as a village close to a city? Or a large natural area on the outskirts of a city?

5. It is important to feel a sense of belonging, to feel that you are an integral part of a community. Do you naturally and easily talk to people and make friends? Are you more of an introvert or extrovert? Are you a joiner? Will you be able to create a new community of friends in your new location if you don't already have one established? If all this is very difficult, choose a location where you already have family or friends.

6. Where is it possible to do what you love to do: consider paid and/ or volunteer work, leisure, and learning options. You don't need to have everything decided now but do know what's possible and what is not, and if you're comfortable being flexible and open to specific opportunities once you've relocated.

7. How far do you want to commute to work? How close do you want to be to an airport for travel?

8. How important is it to be close to ageing parents? Are you the only potential advocate/ caregiver

should the need arise? Do you choose that role for yourself? Are you willing to go to them from wherever you are when/if needed?

When and how to start retirement planning

Know that retirement planning is life planning for your next life stage. Retirement does not mean you're in decline. The new retirement in this age of longevity means re-invention and renewal. It's an opportunity to keep what you love and prune what you no longer want or need in your life, and to carry on living your personal journey.

Considerations and questions to ask yourself:

1. Start now. It's never too early or too late.

2. Think of retirement as a career transition. It's not an ending; it's a new beginning.

3. Consider taking a virtual sabbatical before choosing anything. Give yourself the time you need to consider, explore, and try out your options.

4. Move to a new location on a trial basis and experience what it's like to live there in all seasons before buying or selling a home.

5. If your employer is amenable, gradually reduce your workload from five to four to three or two days per week. Consider mentoring new recruits or taking on a project to work on with reduced hours.

6. Know your values, your personality, interests, skills, wants, and needs. Read *Retire to the Life You Love: Practical Tools for Designing Your Meaningful Future* for a self-help book to guide you.

7. Think beyond work and leisure. Your new life stage provides opportunities to choose to Just Be (for creative and spiritual renewal), Be Compassionate (for kind and loving relationships, including with yourself), Be Well (for health), Be Curious (for continued learning), and Be a Contributor (for paid or volunteer work), or any combination of all five for a rich, full life. You may need to start with Be Well and Just Be if you're exhausted or burned out.

8. Read the self-help guide separately and discuss your thoughts and ideas with your partner. The book gives you the vocabulary you need to start a conversation on any of these topics.

9. Consider this life stage as an opportunity for spiritual growth, for using your extensive life experience, knowledge and skills to contribute to the greater good of society, one person, one thought and one action at a time. You have much to give as a cohort of wise elders on this planet that can help shift any negative energies to positive ones.

10. With thanks to Gandhi, and from one elder to another, please consider choosing to *be* the change you wish to see in the world.

The stages of retirement

Retiring constitutes change. With every external change, you can expect to go through an internal transition that typically has three stages.

The first stage is indeed an ending of your current work as you know it. This is not the end of your life, however. Your task is to simply acknowledge the feelings that come with the ending and know they are normal. You are not the first or the only one having those exact feelings that could range from fear to excitement and that can change from day to day.

As you move into the second phase of transition, you may feel confused and directionless, especially if you have not yet prepared for the change. You can do that now by assessing who you are, your interests, skills, wants, needs, and passions and taking the time to discover a range of options for the life you want to live next.

Once you have a number of options you'd like to consider, start exploring them. Talk to people and try them out. You can think of this phase as a research or pilot project. The important thing here is to take a first step. As you start to take action, you will feel more energised, motivated, and hopeful. Tell everyone you meet what you're interested in and want to know more about and you will be pleasantly surprised at the new connections, resources, and opportunities that emerge.

Through this process you will discover that retiring from a job or career is not the end of your life, but a whole new beginning full of potential for a fulfilling next chapter.

Ruth Van Reken is a US citizen who grew up in Nigeria as a second generation Third Culture Kid (TCK) and then raised her three daughters in Liberia. For over 30 years, Ruth has travelled extensively, speaking about issues related to global family lifestyles. Currently, she seeks to understand how lessons learned from the TCK experience apply to others raised among many cultural worlds for various reasons. Ruth is co-author of *Third Culture Kids: Growing Up Among Worlds, 3rd ed.*, multiple other writings, and co-founder and past chairperson of Families in Global Transition. Ruth and her husband, David, live in Indianapolis

To find out more, visit: www.crossculturalkid.org

Topics covered by Ruth: *Delayed adolescence, Distant relatives, Death of distant relatives, Still moving in our 50s, Making a house a home, Leaving the exotic behind, Guilt, Fitting in, Belonging to a faith community, Prayer and intention, Sibling dynamics, The value of having a forever home, Family traditions, Dynamics with your children's partners, Ageing Parents, Interfaith understanding, Unresolved Grief, How to talk to others in times of grief, Transition of TCK to adulthood.*

Delayed adolescence

Uneven maturity is a common TCK characteristic, with many TCKs wise beyond their years during childhood. As parents, you assume these capable, competent children will be 'just fine' going off to uni, and are shocked to realise your children still need significant support. Even for those who know that TCKs frequently experience 'delayed adolescence', they never expected that it also included their children who were doing so well! But for most TCKs, beginning college or finding a job away from parents is also when they undergo the great challenge of 'repatriation'. You can offer practical support through social media, care packages and so on, and if your TCKs can't return to you for vacations, make sure they have somewhere local to go.

But don't forget: prevention is part of the cure. Learning about normal transition and tips for how to best prepare may not prevent every challenge, but it can reduce the sense of shame or guilt for both you and your TCKs when hard days come. *Third Culture Kids: Growing Up Among Worlds, 3rd ed.* includes a section on transition and tips for parents regarding reentry. *The Global Nomad's Guide to University Transition* by Tina Quick offers step by step guidance for the TCKs themselves.

Distant relatives

It's hard when relatives we love need our support and we aren't there to help. It is excruciating, however, when they are also our children. How do we come to terms with the pain and guilt we feel that our lifestyle has potentially caused their suffering?

But maybe we first need a different question. *Should* we 'come to terms' with these things? Families living apart seem like a 'new normal', but we are only beginning to understand the long-term effects of these chronic cycles of separation and loss on the children. Instead of assuming this lifestyle is inevitably part of the expat experience, could we think radically and consider other options? Are there new paradigms that allow parents with international careers to live both globally and locally according to their children's needs? Already many mission organisations re-assign parents to jobs in the passport country when their children begin attending university. Other expats localise for a time so they can be nearer while launching their children into young adulthood. Could some careers flourish with a mix of internet interactions and occasional travel? There are many possibilities for how we can do expat life better. Let's think creatively!

Death of distant relatives – how to cope and grieve

Death is always hard, but in the expat life, layers are added to that grief. When our dearly loved relative dies, she is thousands of miles away. No one in our expat community knows her so they cannot reminisce with us about her. Despite their words of sympathy, we grieve alone. At 'home' for the funeral, we are relieved to cry with those who share our grief, but then we return to our current posting. Our loss now seems surreal. It's easy to ignore the grief and move on, but then we find ourselves angry or depressed. We need to remember that death is another type of transition and apply what we already know about transitioning to this situation too. Chapter 5 in *Third Culture Kids*, 3rd ed., reminds us to not overlook the inevitable hidden losses that fuel ongoing grief. Some expat communities have periodic 'rituals of mourning'. All who wish to remember their loved one in a communal way take turns writing the person's name on a flip chart, lighting a candle while offering words of remembrance or a prayer before sitting. Having some physical ceremony is helpful, even if with just one friend.

Still moving in our 50s

Ageing is an interesting process that seems to catch us unaware. We have looked at those older than ourselves as 'them', but they will surely never be 'us'. Ageing on the move adds another layer. For expats, life transitions such as children leaving home, parents needing care or dying, often coincide with this early ageing time. Suddenly the questions of, "When do I stop moving? And where do I then go?" become real – and a bit frightening. We wonder, *If travelling seems such a part of who I am, who will I be if I stop moving? Will I still be me?* This is a critical time in life to double check our basic sense of identity and to continue discovering what it means to be 'me'. *Who am I as a person and what are my distinct gifts and calling that make me* this *person?* Then, whether we move or stay, we can find contentment for our circumstances no longer define us. Chapter 6 in *Third Culture Kids* discusses how looking at 'likeness' and 'uniqueness' helps us find our identity in this way.

Making a house a home

Because place is a key factor in the question of belonging and identity, it's vitally important that we create spaces for emotional connection as well as physical protection and provision. This is why 'sacred objects' are so important. As we put familiar pictures on the wall, set up family photos on the dresser, or bring in the favorite couch from the moving van, life begins to feel more normal. One person I met paints all her walls the same sage green everywhere she goes. That, plus the pictures she hangs up, creates a magical sense of home for her family. It is also important we create 'home' through non-physical entities: re-establishing family routines; reading a familiar bedtime story to young kids; planning meals that include favourite recipes from past places; or doing family activities similar to what we did before. Never forget that for many TCKs, the sense of home is most often defined in terms of relationships, not place per se. Recreating the environment and continuing the types of things done before as a family usually mean there is still a place of retreat and belonging for each family member, even if the outside world is completely changed.

Leaving the exotic behind

Not easy. Often we give many other excuses for why we can't stop, but the truth is we can get almost addicted to our global lifestyle. It may be one way of coping, while we ignore other things in our lives. But it is also true that despite the busyness and exhausting relocations, it is a fun and interesting way to live. How else would we interact with so many interesting cultures or geographic wonders? Where else might we meet so many amazing people with all their fascinating, global stories?

Yes, it can be hard to give up this lifestyle even when we know our parents or children need us. We fear monotony and the blandness of a more monocultural existence. Here are some tips for when that time comes. Mourn the obvious and hidden losses of this change well. Build Dave

Pollock's RAFT of Reconciliation, Affirmation, Farewells and Thinking destination as you leave (you can find this in *Third Culture Kids* but it is also widely available on the Internet). Remember you are still you, no matter where you are. Dare to explore the adventure of staying in one place for a while. Some things grow deeper when not being constantly replanted. It's a change but not all bad!

Guilt

First question: are we talking about guilt or shame? Years ago, I heard a very helpful distinction between them. The speaker said, "Guilt is for when you do something morally wrong. The antidote for that is forgiveness. Shame is for who you are. The only antidote for that is grace." This was transformative for me. Now when that dreadful sense of failure or deepest regret comes, I ask myself: *Is this guilt or shame I'm feeling?* If I have sinned, there is legitimate guilt and a healthy shame. I need to ask forgiveness from God, others or myself. Usually, however, I am feeling the shame that I made a mistake or didn't do something perfectly, particularly when I see my children struggle. All the *I should* and *I shouldn't* messages crowd in and curl me into a foetal position inside. But there is always a lie in shame, and the lie here is that somehow I could have known all the ramifications of my decision beforehand. The truth is if I *had* that power, I would have made different decisions but I don't. Instead of being all knowing, like God, I am a fallible, limited human being. Accepting that reality is extending grace to myself and receiving it from others.

Fitting in

Like all children, most TCKs want to fit in. In the culturally-mixed environment of an international school, this is not so hard where difference among peers is the norm, at least in terms of ethnicity, nationality, dress, or what foods they carry in their lunch box.

But when TCKs repatriate to a more homogenous environment, things change and TCKs have several common responses. Some become *chameleons*, wanting to hide any differences and they work hard to fit by being 'the same as'. The *screamers*, by contrast, adopt a 'different from' identity and boldly proclaim it by hairstyle, clothing, attitude or whatever. Some choose to be *wallflowers*, staying by the edges where it feels safer than running the risk of making a cultural mistake in this new world. Then, of course, we have the *adapters*. For whatever reason, they seem to have a strong enough sense of internal identity to move ahead, apparently without worrying whether they do or don't fit in. While these reactions are initially normal, helping children develop a sense of personal identify is key to long-term success. See Chapter 6 of *Third Culture Kids: Growing Up Among Worlds* for more details on the challenges to identity formation for TCKs and how to help.

Belonging to a faith community

For many, belonging to a faith community deeply enriches our expat experience. Traditionally, such communities gathered primarily in churches, temples and mosques and shared the historical tenets of their respective religions. In today's world, some gather in health clubs or similar places where they share their faith in a more generic form of spirituality, often rooted in the tradition of Eastern religious practices. Mindfulness may replace prayer and yoga may replace a more traditional 'quiet time', but in all of these groups there is a shared belief system in the deeper layers of our beings. Finding such a community with others of many cultures and nationalities, amid a sea of changing cultural norms in the larger world around us, offers a true sense of coming 'home'. Why? Because, despite our different backgrounds, we see the world around us through the shared lenses of our faith. In such a community, others understand when we talk about our sense of spiritual realities and offer hope as they share their stories of how this shared faith has strengthened their lives in return. It's a good place to be!

Prayer and intention

As a Christian, prayer has been a vital part of my life. Often it is simply an ongoing 'chatting' with God as I do daily life. It also includes designated 'quiet times' – those moments I intentionally stop for prayer and meditation on Scripture. It is here I sit and listen as well as speak to God and process life, wrestling with the deepest travails of my soul, expressing my doubts, my fears, my thanks and my joys, and knowing I can be honest before God. Sometimes I write out my prayers when my thoughts whirl in circles. In these moments, I also receive comfort and guidance for my life.

That's my story but I also realise everyone does not share the same beliefs as I do regarding prayer. I have heard many talks on 'intention' or mindfulness that sound similar to prayer or meditation. When I hear people talk about releasing 'energy' or 'sending energy', it sounds similar to what I call a 'prayer request': asking for help or blessing. I am not wise enough to explain the mysteries of the spiritual realms of our universe, but I do believe humans of all generations have felt the need to connect with the one I call God, others may call it a Higher Power or the Universe, and prayer and intention are two ways we do that.

Sibling dynamics

A tough issue expats face is when one child seems to be 'flying', within the context of a globally nomadic childhood, while another seems to be drowning. Parents wonder: *What did we do wrong? Why is one doing so well and not the other? Is it their fault or ours?* The sibling who is flying feels impatient; *We've all lived the same life. What's their problem?* And for the ones who struggle, shame reigns; *What's the matter with me? Why can't I be like them?*

Before blame is assigned, remember that each child has lived a unique life. Families move at different times in each child's development process. There are key ages when moving is easiest on the child (infant in arms) or hardest (pre and early teen years). The timing of moves and who was and wasn't able to make a good friend in each move can change the dynamic for each child. This means that, as parents, we cannot compare our children but must seek to understand each one's personality and story. What nurtures their souls? How can we listen well to the joys they feel as well as the sadnesses? Read Robin Pascoe's book *Raising Global Nomads* for more parenting tips.

The value of having a forever home

While expat living is often exciting, we know frequent moves take an incredible amount of energy. For many years, taking young children here and there seemed part of our family adventures. Then they begin to move out of our home and begin to scatter. We, too, are getting older and begin to wonder how long we can live life on the move. At this point, having a physical space to come back to becomes important. Where will the family consistently gather when scattered across the globe? Where will the grandchildren visit at holidays? How do we make this happen? Place is important, and the sense of 'coming home' is one of life's silent joys. How do we make this happen?

Some families keep a house in the passport country so their children can come back to the same place, same bedroom and same neighbourhood each leave. When the time to stop travelling comes, the choice of where to go is relatively simple. For most, however, establishing a permanent base depends on many factors such as being near relatives, job opportunities, even health needs. Yes, establishing a 'forever home' is important and critical at some point in our journeys as our personal and family needs evolve.

Family traditions

Family is the one place many TCKs identify as their primary place of belonging. "I am at home wherever my family is." Because family is the transportable 'home base' of global living, traditions that can also be transported are key in helping to establish family identity. These are the things we do as this particular family no matter where we are, no matter how else people do things. This is 'us'. The traditions can be simple: a favorite food for Ramadan or other holidays, personalised Christmas stockings hung wherever seems most like a fireplace, or a special Hanukkah candle-holder set up in the current window. For globally mobile families, incorporating some of the local traditions into the family's traditions also reminds us of the unique history of our journey together. In Liberia the song *Green Christmas* wafted through the air each December. We played during family celebrations at Christmas long after we had repatriated. It reminded us of the joys we had known there, and the sadnesses that had since come to our beloved land. Yes, traditions are important!

Dynamics with our children's partners

The first time we realise our precious child may soon give more loyalty and time to this new love, rather than to us, is a bit shocking! A few thoughts from one who has done this three times.

First, don't panic that you are about to 'lose' your child. A wise woman once offered this advice: "Ruth, you have to learn to 're-family' at every stage of life. When your kids go to college, when they marry, when the first grandchild comes, your family dynamics will change. Remember, you aren't losing the past, but looking for ways to re-family for the present and future." This includes sharing your child with his or her in-laws!

Second, if you have cautions, be wise in how you call attention to them. While dating a young man in high school, my father simply said one day, "Ruth, if you marry him, of course we will accept him completely. But if you do, consider you may always have to do things his way, and don't see him doing things your way." Overtly, I disagreed but inside I started to pay attention… and he was right!

Third, let them 'leave and cleave'. They may make mistakes but they will learn as you did. Bless them on their journey, support all you can… and keep your advice to a minimum.

Ageing parents

More and more expats are facing the reality of caring for ageing parents. This is a sobering moment, particularly for those still on the go. How will careers be affected if travel is curtailed? What about caring for our kids on the other end of the spectrum? How do we put it all together? In these moments, we realise anew that life isn't only and always about us. After our wonderful global adventures, life will potentially change to a more local adventure: caring for parents in their later years. Certainly not an easy transition, even if a right one. But it can be done. Yes, I grieved when I realised my mother, who was living with us, could no longer care for herself and I would have to stop most of my travels. In this transition, I wrote down my obvious and hidden losses and mourned this change from freedom to caregiver. Caregiving lasted four and a half years, but I am grateful that she could die in our 'forever home' surrounded by family and love. Other options include repatriating near the parents, working out a plan for siblings to help, or sending money to help pay for professional care when you or others are not able to be there.

Interfaith understanding and the TCK openness

Among the many paradoxes in the TCK experience is the impact of exposure to multiple faiths. Having friends with very different faith backgrounds, and often living in a culture totally shaped by a different religion than what they may practise, is a gift. Contrary to common stereotypes of 'them', TCKs learn quickly that those judged as 'different' because of their beliefs are not to be feared. They know these 'others' are persons who, like themselves, laugh, cry, think, want friends and to be understood. The paradox, however, relates to what Barbara Schaetti writes in her groundbreaking PhD work on TCK identities (https://www.worldweave.com/BSidentity.html).

She stresses the need for TCKs to have a stable spiritual core by knowing what she calls 'their truth' – what they believe and value no matter where they live. But how do they sort out their beliefs from the many they have seen? Some say, "Don't worry. All religions are basically the same." But when TCKs know more deeply each religion's tenets, that statement is logically impossible as the beliefs in one religion often contradict another's. Once they sort this out, however, most are able to own their beliefs clearly while respecting those who differ from them.

Unresolved grief

This topic is far too complicated to explain in a couple of paragraphs, but I believe it is the number one issue I see in ATCKs who are struggling. They may presume their problem is depression or anger or anxiety, but behind it is grief. So many cycles of mobility create a large number of losses regardless of what we also gain. While grief is a normal part of life when we lose things we love, the question is why it so often remains unresolved for those who are relocating physically. There can be several reasons for this:

- Lack of awareness

- Lack of permission

- Lack of time

- Lack of comfort

To understand this issue in the depth it deserves, please read Chapter 5 of *Third Culture Kids: Growing Up Among Worlds* and/ or the appendix that Lois Bushong wrote on grief for *Raising Global Nomads,* by Robin Pascoe. Therapists will also find Lois's book, *Belonging Everywhere and Nowhere: Counseling the Globally Mobile,* a great help.

How to talk to others at times of grief

Each time we have loss, we experience grief. Helping others through their grief means recognising their loss and giving permission, time and comfort for the grief process to happen. Start by paying attention to symptoms such as depression, anxiety or excessive anger. These may be symptoms of grief. Start there. If we ask our son why he is sad, he may say, "We just moved." Instead of telling him why this new place is wonderful, give him permission to sit with that sadness. "That must have been hard. What are you saddest about in leaving?" Perhaps he will say "Playing soccer". Explore again: "What will you miss most about playing soccer?" Your son may go say the obvious, "My friends," but you might gently ask, "Is soccer a place where you felt like you belonged at your school?" This helps him name a more hidden loss. Often this is where the tears will come. Then comfort, acknowledging that it is hard to lose. Above all, do not compare his situation to someone else's. Nothing shuts down the process of grief faster than that. If you enter into his (or someone else's grief), he will in time emerge and usually move on to the good still ahead.

Transition of TCK to adulthood

Wow, what a broad topic! Some TCKs make this journey exhibiting all the strengths of the TCK experience. They are multi-lingual, good communicators and cultural bridges with a wonderful sense of ease no matter the situation. For whatever reason, they have a strong sense of personal identity and this transition is smooth.

Sadly, others struggle big time. Delayed adolescence is one factor. Because normal patterns of cultural learning were frequently interrupted by mobility during childhood, TCKs don't always know how the adult world operates. They haven't had entry-level jobs in high school where some early lessons about adult roles are learned. Many don't know how to translate life skills they learned overseas to another environment.

Parents should not despair. Their TCKs may be slower to launch than expected, but TCKs can learn. With coaching and perhaps establishing a 'forever home', confidence can grow. Another new paradigm, however, is accepting that for some TCKs finding a job or way to return to the international community where they do know how things work, can contribute their gifts, and feel they belong, can be part of the answer. Parents may be surprised but it works for them and uses the life their parents gave them.

BIBLIOGRAPHY

ARTICLES

'Mothers' and Fathers' Perceptions of Change and Continuity in Their Relationships With Young Adult Sons and Daughters', Christine Proulx and Heather Helms, *Journal of Family Issues*, 1 August 2007. Available at: https://pdfs.semanticscholar.org/140c/2b3ff5752ddfddf18a8eca20845383c05bce.pdf

'Young, Underemployed and Optimistic: Coming of Age, Slowly, in a Tough Economy', *Pew Research Center*, 9 February 2012. Available at:

www.pewsocialtrends.org/2012/02/09/young-underemployed-and-optimistic/

PUBLICATIONS

A Career In Your Suitcase, 4th Ed. Jo Parfitt and Colleen Reichrath-Smith, published by Summertime Publishing, 2013.

An Inconvenient Posting – An Expat Wife's Memoir of Lost Identity, Laura J. Stephens, published by Springtime Books, 2012.

Belonging Everywhere and Nowhere: Counseling the Globally Mobile, Lois Bushong, published by Mango Tree Intercultural Services, 2013.

Beyond the Mommy Year: How to Live Happily Ever After... After the Kids Leave Home, Carin Rubenstein, PhD, published by Grand Central Publishing, 2008.

Can Any Mother Help Me? Jenna Bailey, published by Faber & Faber, 2012.

Designing Your Life: How to Build a Well-Lived, Joyful Life, Bill Burnett and Dave Evans, published by Knopf Doubleday Publishing Group, 2016.

Emerging Adulthood: The Winding Road from the Late Teens Through the Early Twenties, Jeffrey Jensen Arnett, published by Oxford University Press, 2004.

Emotional Resilience and the Expat Child: Practical Tips and Storytelling Techniques that will Strengthen the Global Family, Julia Simens, published by Summertime Publishing, 2011.

Five Flights Up, Kristin Louise Duncombe, published by CreateSpace, 2016.

Global Mom, Melissa Dalton-Bradford, published by Familius, 2017.

Harvesting Stones, Paula Lucas, published by Summertime Publishing, 2013.

Hierarchy of Needs: A Theory of Human Motivation, Abraham H. Maslow, published in *Psychological Review*, 1943.

Irresistible: The Rise of Addictive Technology and the Business of Keeping Us Hooked, Adam Alter, published by Penguin Press, 2017.

Managing Transitions: Making the Most of Change, William Bridges, published by Addison-Wesley, 1991.

Parenting From the Inside Out: How A Deeper Self-Understanding Can Help You Raise Children Who Thrive, Daniel Siegel and Mary Hartzell, published by Penguin Putnam Inc, 2005.

Passages: Predictable Crises of Adult Life, Gail Sheehy, published by Bantam Books and EP Dutton and Co Inc, 1976.

Raising Global Nomads, Robin Pascoe, published by Expatriate Press Limited, 2006.

Retire to the Life You Love, Practical Tools for Designing Your Meaningful Future, Nell Smith, published by Summertime Publishing, 2014.

Safe Passage, Douglas W Ota, published by Summertime Publishing, 2014.

Sunshine Soup, Jo Parfitt, published by Summertime Publishing, 2011.

The Artist's Way Julia Cameron, published by Penguin USA, 1992.

The Desire Map, Danielle Laporte, published by Sounds True Inc, 2014.

The Emotionally Resilient Expat: Engage, Adapt and Thrive Across Cultures, published by Summertime Publishing, 2013.

The Global Nomad's Guide To University Transition, Tina Quick, published by Summertime Publishing, 2011.

The Mobile Life: A New Approach to Moving Anywhere, Diane Lemieux and Anne Parker, published by Scriptum Books, 2014.

The Physics of Living, Norm Amundson, published by Ergon Communications, 2003.

The Prophet, Khalil Gibran, published by Alfred A. Knopf, 1923.

The Right to Write, Julia Cameron, published by G.P. Putnam's Sons, 1998.

The Seven Habits of Highly Effective People, Steven R. Covey, published by Free Press, 1989.

The Stone Bridal Bed, Harry Mulisch, published by Aberlard-Schuman, 1959.

Third Culture Kids: Growing Up Among Worlds, Ruth Van Reken and David C. Pollock, published by Nicholas Brealey Publishing, 2001.

Trailing – A Memoir, Kristin Louise Duncombe, published by CreateSpace, 2012.

Transitions, Making Senses of Life's Changes, William Bridges, published by De Capo Lifelong Books, 2004.

Untethered Soul – Journey Beyond Yourself, Michael A. Singer, published by New Harbinger Publications/Noetic Books 2007.

Work With Passion, Nancy Anderson, published by Avalon Publishing Group, 1984.

Writing Down the Bones: Freeing the Writer Within, Natalie Goldberg, published by Shambhala, 2006.

Writing in a Convertible with the Top Down, Shelia Bender and Christi Killien, published by Blue Heron Publishing.

OTHER

Could Writing Be Your Portable Career? visit www. summertimepublishing.com/blog/category/jo-parfitt

Desert Island Discs, Sheryl Sandberg, visit www.bbc.co.uk/programmes/b08z9b81

Green Christmas, visit
https://www.youtube.com/watch?v=I5IXlfJSEi4

Henry V, William Shakespeare, visit
www.shakespeareonline.com/plays/henryvscenes.html

Riverdale, visit https://www.netflix.com/title/80133311

The Arrangement, visit www.imdb.com/title/tt4941288/

The Weekly Telegraph, visit www.telegraph.co.uk

Transitions Abroad, visit www.transitionsabroad.com

When We Are Married, visit https://www.raretv2dvd.co.uk/product-page/when-we-are-married-j-b-priestley

10X Your Productivity, workshop by Blanca Vergara, visit www.blancavergara.com

WEB LINKS

www.careerinyoursuitcase.com

www.crossculturalkid.org

http://culture3counsel.com/

https://en.wikipedia.org/wiki/SWOT_analysis

www.headspace.org.au

https://www.iirp.edu/what-we-do/what-is-restorative-practices/defining-restorative/22-5-3-family-group-conference-fgc-or-family-group-decision-making-fgdm

www.laurenbramleymd.com

https://mensshed.org

www.mentoring.org

www.praanawellness.com

www.rnginternational.com

http://www.worldweave.com

https://www.worldweave.com/BSidentity.html

Wilson Family in India 2018

Wilson Family in Qatar 1996

ABOUT THE AUTHORS

TERRY ANNE WILSON

"At the age of 26, I carried off my hopes and dreams in a 55-litre backpack, embarking on a six-month trek through Asia. Copious letters were written back to Canada and my adventures journaled in loving detail. Writing has always been a way of connecting with others and capturing my experiences for posterity. And now, a deep love of history, people and culture infuses my work as I travel and live globally.

I have walked much of that path with my travel companion and husband of 27 years and our three sons, each born in a different land. We currently live in India, the ninth country that we've called home.

From Teacher to Cultural Trainer to Tour Guide/ Historian, I ultimately discovered my passion – as a writer and a researcher. I share my journey through my blog, hoping to convey a cultural and historical context to our world. My first co-authored book *Pioneers of Penang*, affirmed my love of historical writing. *Monday Morning Emails* speaks to the power of writing and of claiming your personal stories. It seems that things have come full circle – this book will sit proudly alongside those old travel journals!"

You can find out more about me at:

terryannewilson@mac.com

https://wordpress.com/posts/notesonaboardingpass.wordpress.com

Instagram: @notesonaboardingpass

Parfitt Family in Borneo 2012

Parfitt Family in Oman 1994

JO PARFITT

"Like many of us, I have embraced social media and Smartphones and use both to keep in touch. As a writer, this is second nature. I've written books (this will be my 32nd), articles, poems, blogs, training courses, brochures, letters and emails over the 30 years I have accompanied my husband, Ian, on a series of eight moves. We left England for Dubai in 1987 where we had our sons, Sam and Joshua. From there we moved to Oman, then Stavanger, back to England, over to The Hague, briefly Brunei, Kuala Lumpur and now find ourselves back in The Hague.

Throughout this time I have continued to work as a writer, publisher, teacher and writers' mentor and run residential Writing Me-Treats worldwide. It's been and continues to be fun yet I admit it can be darn tough too.

Writing this book and the emails from which it grew has been a revelation, deeply fulfilling and a joy. Social media has its place but please let's revive the art of writing letters."

You can find out more about me at:

www.joparfitt.com

www.summertimepublishing.com

www.springtimebooks.com

www.expatbookshop.com

www.writingmetreats.com

Would you and a friend like to write a book for our Morning Email series?

Would you like to work with Jo Parfitt and the team at Summertime Publishing and receive big royalties?

Then please email in the first instance to: jo@summertimepublishing.com

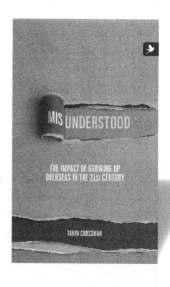

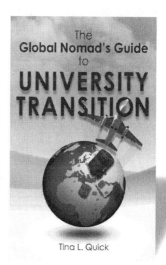

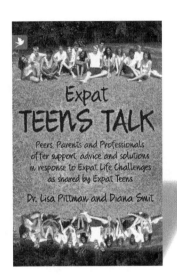

Expat
TEENS TALK

Peers, Parents and Professionals
offer support, advice and solutions
in response to Expat Life Challenges
as shared by Expat Teens

Dr. Lisa Pittman and Diana Smit

my
Moving Booklet

We will miss you very much
and wish you all the best
on your new adventures!

created by
Valérie
Besanceney

B at Home

Emma
Moves
again

By Valérie
Besanceney

SLURPING SOUP
and other confusions:

INSIGHTS AND INTERVIEWS FROM
**THE 2014
FAMILIES IN
GLOBAL TRANSITION
(FIGT) CONFERENCE**
THE GLOBAL FAMILY REDEFINED

Edited by Jo Parfitt
with Sue Mannering and
Dounia Bertuccelli

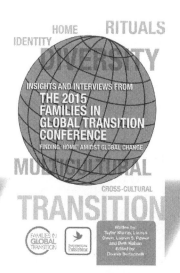

INSIGHTS AND INTERVIEWS FROM
**THE 2015
FAMILIES IN
GLOBAL TRANSITION
CONFERENCE**
FINDING 'HOME' AMIDST GLOBAL CHANGE

Written by:
Taylor Murray, Lauren
Owen, Lauren S. Power
and Beth Haban
Edited by:
Dounia Bertuccelli

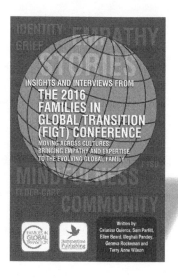

INSIGHTS AND INTERVIEWS FROM
**THE 2016
FAMILIES IN
GLOBAL TRANSITION
(FIGT) CONFERENCE**
MOVING ACROSS CULTURES:
BRINGING EMPATHY AND EXPERTISE
TO THE EVOLVING GLOBAL FAMILY

Written by:
Catarina Queiroz, Sam Parfitt,
Ellen Beard, Meghali Pandey,
Geneva Rockeman and
Terry Anne Wilson

INSIGHTS AND INTERVIEWS FROM
**THE 2017
FAMILIES IN
GLOBAL TRANSITION
(FIGT) CONFERENCE**
BUILDING ON THE BASICS:
CREATING YOUR TRIBE ON THE MOVE

Written By: Tone Delin Indrelid,
Jane Barron, Mariam Ottimofiore
and Sarah Janney Stoner with
Glony Philips, Sarah Black, Carolyn
Parse Rizzo and Sara Coggiola
Edited by: Dounia Bertuccelli

A Global Nomad's Journey From Hurt To Healing

Letters

NEVER SENT

RUTH E. VAN REKEN

MORE THAN 32,000 COPIES SOLD

"Truly inspirational for any mobile individual." Expatriate Adviser

Jo Parfitt & Colleen Reichrath-Smith

a career
in your suitcase

A practical guide to creating meaningful work... anywhere

4th Edition

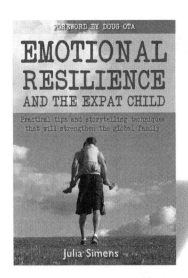

FOREWORD BY DOUG OTA

EMOTIONAL
RESILIENCE
AND THE EXPAT CHILD

Practical tips and storytelling techniques
that will strengthen the global family

Julia Simens

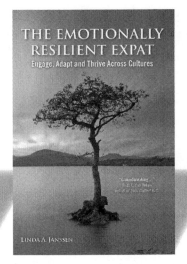

THE EMOTIONALLY
RESILIENT EXPAT
Engage, Adapt and Thrive Across Cultures

"Groundbreaking..."
Ruth E. Van Reken,
co-author of Third Culture Kids

LINDA A. JANSSEN

A REUNION
OF STRANGERS

.Words of Wisdom from the
FAMILIES IN GLOBAL TRANSITION
Conference Community

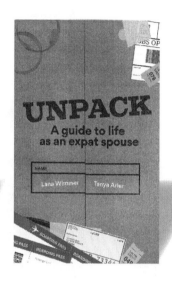

UNPACK
A guide to life
as an expat spouse

NAME

Lana Wimmer   Tanya Arler

Retire to the Life You Love

Practical Tools for Designing Your Meaningful Future

Nell Smith

AN
INCONVENIENT
POSTING

Laura J Stephens

Contact INFO

RNG International
383 Corona Street
Suite 300
Denver, CO 80218

Phone: **720-627-6940**
info@rnginternational.com

Our areas of expertise INCLUDE

✓ Traditional and specialized boarding schools

✓ University application and admission advising

✓ Learning differences and ADD concerns, including evaluations

✓ Gifted and talented children

✓ Therapeutic placements for struggling teens

✓ Choosing the right international school

✓ Public speaking engagements

✓ Transition issues for internationally mobile families

REBECCA GRAPPO, M.ED,
Certified Educational Planner

MICHELLE GRAPPO, M.A., ED.M.,
Nationally Certified School Psychologist

educational
GUIDANCE

for students and families
around the world

Designed by

54398398R00200

Made in the USA
Columbia, SC
30 March 2019